JAPANESE KANJI

MNEMONICS

JLPT

N5

JAPANESE KANJI

MNEMONICS

JLPT N5

Lindsay Jimenez
Dioxelis Lopez

2024

ACKNOWLEDGEMENTS

My husband, Dioxelis Lopez, deserves full credit for the writing of this book. Without his help, support, and constructive criticism this project would have stayed in my mind and would never have become a reality. I dedicate this book to him for every little crazy thing he has done for me. I would also like to thank my mother, my father, and my three brothers who have been my biggest inspiration and strength.

Book design by Lindsay Jimenez

Cover design by Harold Jimenez

English editor Anna Shusterman

Formatting by Dioxelis Lopez

Contents

HOW TO USE THIS BOOK

The main goal of this book is to help those who are studying Japanese as a second language. For this reason, the book is centered on a specific Japanese Language Proficiency Test (JLPT) level. This first book, of the Japanese Kanji Mnemonics Series, focuses on the 103 Japanese characters (kanji) found on the N5 level test and it assumes the reader has knowledge of the two Japanese alphabets (Hiragana and Katakana). In order to start using this book, please follow the following steps:

1. FRONT PAGE:
    a. Flashcard Style: The book is recommended to be used as flashcards. Therefore, the student will find the kanji mnemonic on the front page and the kanji information on the other side.
    b. Mnemonic: The drawings have been made to match the characters' radicals, elements and history as much as possible. In the cases where this was not possible, I just tried to make it easy to remember, and cited some notes about the etymology. However, creativity from the reader is also highly encouraged.

2. BACK PAGE:
    a. Common Meaning(s): The student will find the meanings that are most appropriate for the N5 level.
    b. Sentence: A sentence to help remember the kanji better and that also creates a story that can be used as a mnemonic device. Each sentence was formed by breaking down the kanji into different elements for easy memorization.
    c. Stroke Order: The order in which the kanji must be written.
    d. Writing Exercise: The student will have the opportunity to write the kanji in this section of the book for extra practice.
    e. ON and kun readings: These serve as a guide for the student to only focus on learning and practicing the readings that will be required in the exam. Note: When a

particular reading does not fall in either category, it will be noted as *Reading Exception*

f. <u>Examples</u>: In this section of the book, you will find the following:

- Vocabulary: The words chosen for each kanji in this book are words relevant to the JLPT N5. This is to give the student the opportunity to practice vocabulary found in the exam.
- Furigana: All words contain their corresponding furigana on top of each kanji.
- Abbreviations: In the examples you can also find the following abbreviations:
  - adj = Adjective
  - n = Noun
- Advanced Kanji: These words were included as the word itself is required for the exam, yet, the student will not be required to know the advanced kanji.

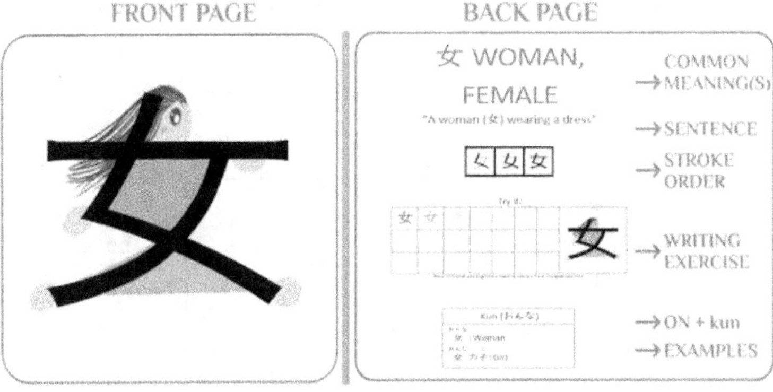

3. This book is not meant to be used on its own. It is highly recommended that the student also uses reading comprehension materials, such a fairy tales or books, as after seeing the different kanji in actual sentences; it will reinforce what was learned in this book.

HIRAGANA CHART

あ a	い i	う u	え e	お o
か ka	き ki	く ku	け ke	こ ko
が ga	ぎ gi	ぐ gu	げ ge	ご go
さ sa	し shi	す su	せ se	そ so
ざ za	じ ji	ず zu	ぜ ze	ぞ zo
た ta	ち chi	つ tsu	て te	と to
だ da	ぢ di	づ du	で de	ど do
な na	に ni	ぬ nu	ね ne	の no
は ha	ひ hi	ふ fu	へ he	ほ ho
ば ba	び bi	ぶ bu	べ be	ぼ bo
ぱ pa	ぴ pi	ぷ pu	ぺ pe	ぽ po
ま ma	み mi	む mu	め me	も mo
や ya		ゆ yu		よ yo
ら ra	り ri	る ru	れ re	ろ ro
わ wa				を wo
ん n				

KATAKANA CHART

ア a	イ i	ウ u	エ e	オ o
カ ka	キ ki	ク ku	ケ ke	コ ko
ガ ga	ギ gi	グ gu	ゲ ge	ゴ go
サ sa	シ shi	ス su	セ se	ソ so
ザ za	ジ ji	ズ zu	ゼ ze	ゾ zo
タ ta	チ chi	ツ tsu	テ te	ト to
ダ da	ヂ di	ヅ du	デ de	ド do
ナ na	ニ ni	ヌ nu	ネ ne	ノ no
ハ ha	ヒ hi	フ fu	ヘ he	ホ ho
バ ba	ビ bi	ブ bu	ベ be	ボ bo
パ pa	ピ pi	プ pu	ペ pe	ポ po
マ ma	ミ mi	ム mu	メ me	モ mo
ヤ ya		ユ yu		ヨ yo
ラ ra	リ ri	ル ru	レ re	ロ ro
ワ wa				ヲ wo
ン n				

STROKE ORDER RULES

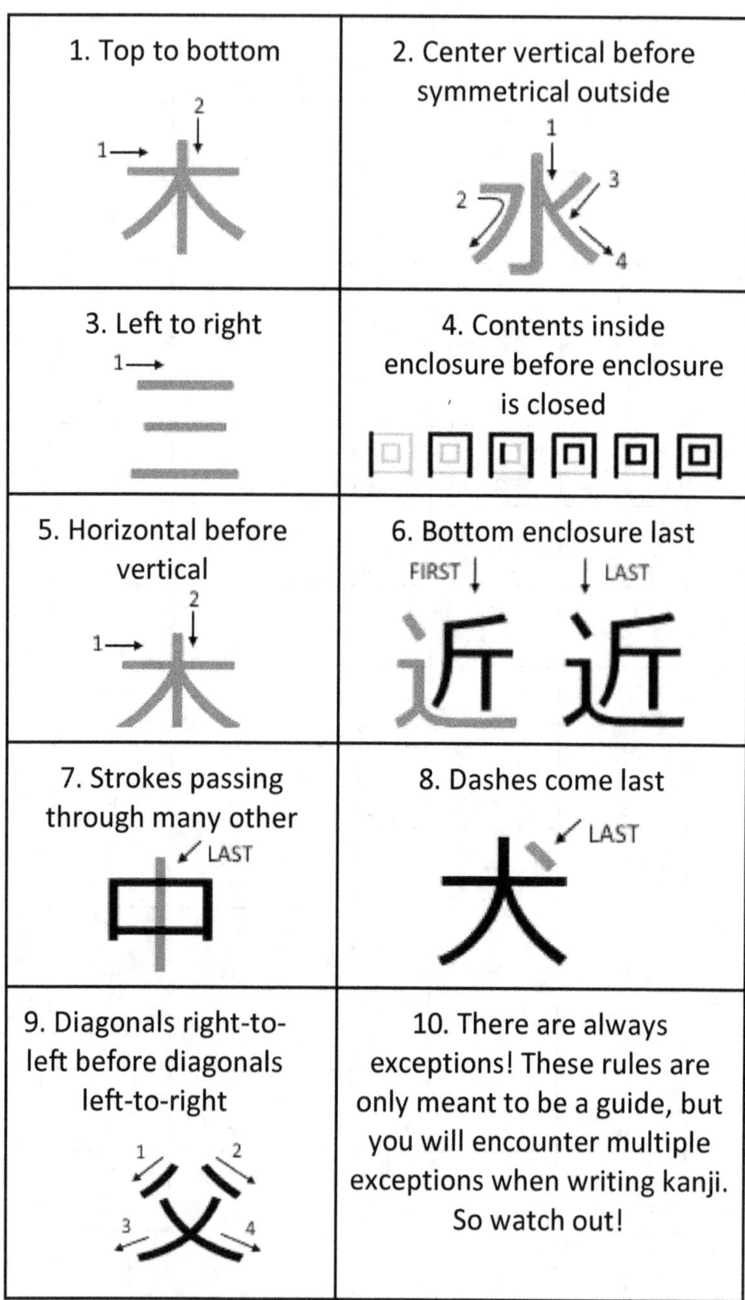

CHAPTER 1: NATURE

日	月	火	水	木
1	2	3	4	5
金	土	本	山	川
6	7	8	9	10
天	空	雨	電	魚
11	12	13	14	15
花	気	国		
16	17	18		

日 SUN, DAY

"A sun (日) and a cloud on a bright day"

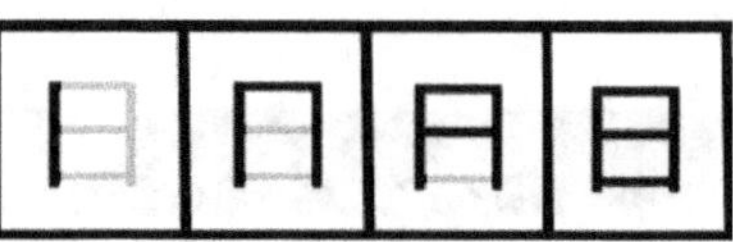

Try it:

ON (ニチ)

いちにち
一 日 : One day, Whole day

まいにち
毎 日 : Every day

Kun (ひ，か)

はつか
二十日 : Twenty days, twentieth

にちようび
日 曜 日 : Sunday

月 MOON, MONTH

"There is a blue moon (月) this month"

月 | 月 | 月 | 月

Try it:

ON (ゲツ、ガツ)
げつようび 月曜日：Monday
こんげつ 今月：This month
せんげつ 先月：Last month
らいげつ 来月：Next month
げつ 〜か月：(Number of) months
がつ 〜月：Month of the year

Kun (つき)
ひとつき 一月：One month
まいつき 毎月：Every month

火 FIRE

"Two fire (火) logs burning"

火 火 火 火

Try it:

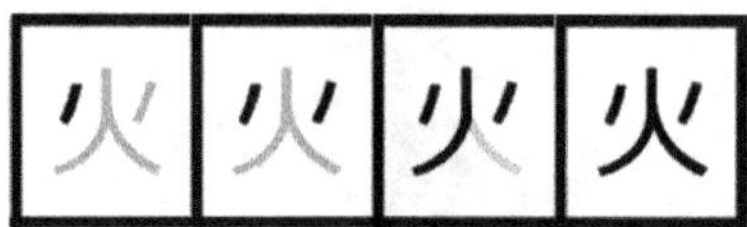

ON (カ)
かようび 火曜日 : Tuesday
かざん 火山 : Volcano
か　じ 火事 : Fire

水 WATER

"The water (水) makes a big splash"

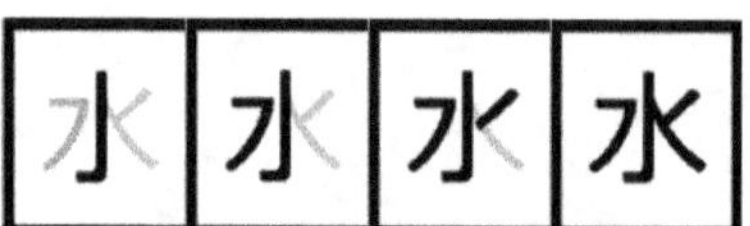

Try it:

ON (スイ)
すいようび 水曜日 : Wednesday

Kun (みず)
みず 水 : Water

木 TREE

"One tree (木) with two branches"

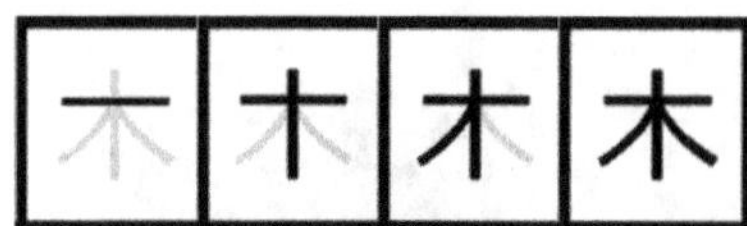

Try it:

ON (モク)

もくようび
木曜日 : Thursday

Kun (き)

き
木 : Tree

金 GOLD

"Two gold (金) nuggets inside the mine"

金 金 金 金
金 金 金 金

Try it:

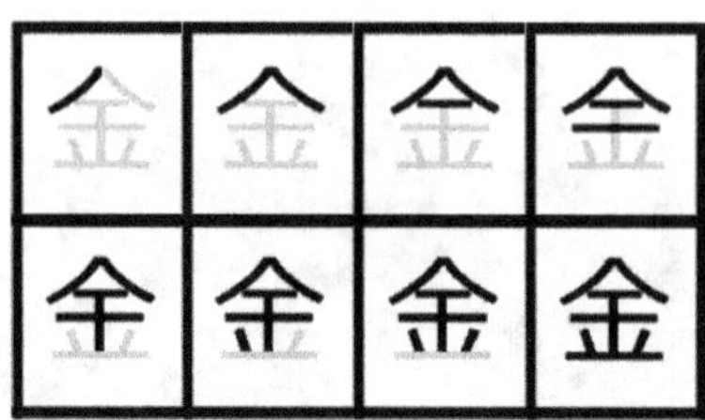

ON (キン)
きんようび
金曜日 : Friday
きんぎょ
金魚 : Goldfish

Kun (かね)
かね
お金 : Money

土 EARTH

"The plants grow from the earth (土)"

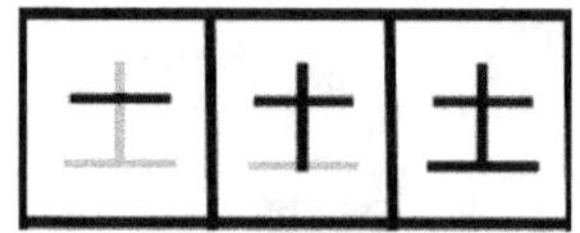

Try it:

ON (ド)		
どようび 土曜日 : Saturday		

Kun (つち)		
つち 土 : Earth, soil		

本 BOOK, ORIGIN

"That book (本) is about the origin of the
Tree of Life"

本 本 本 本 本

Try it:

本 本

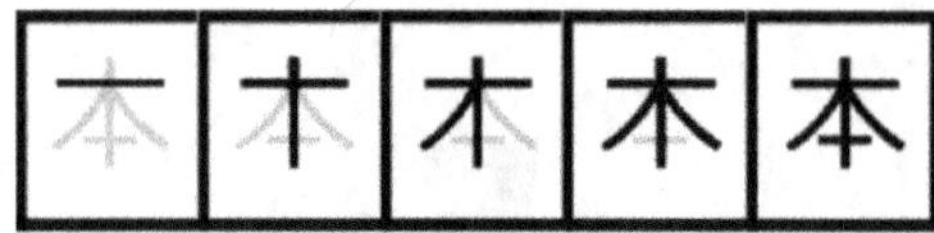

ON (ホン)
ほん 本 : Book
ほんだな 本 棚 : Bookshelves
にほん 日本 : Japan
ほん 〜 本 : Counter for long cylindrical things

山 MOUNTAIN

"The three peaks are the mountains (山)"

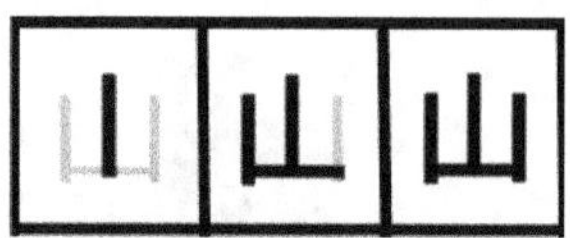

Try it:

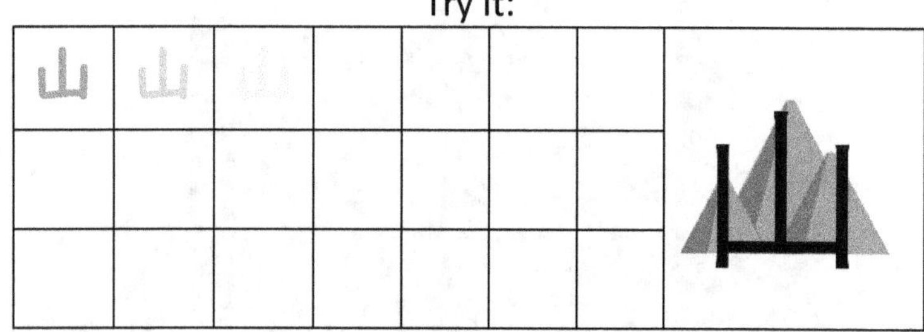

ON (サン)
ふじ 山 : Mountain Fuji

Kun (やま)
山 : Mountain

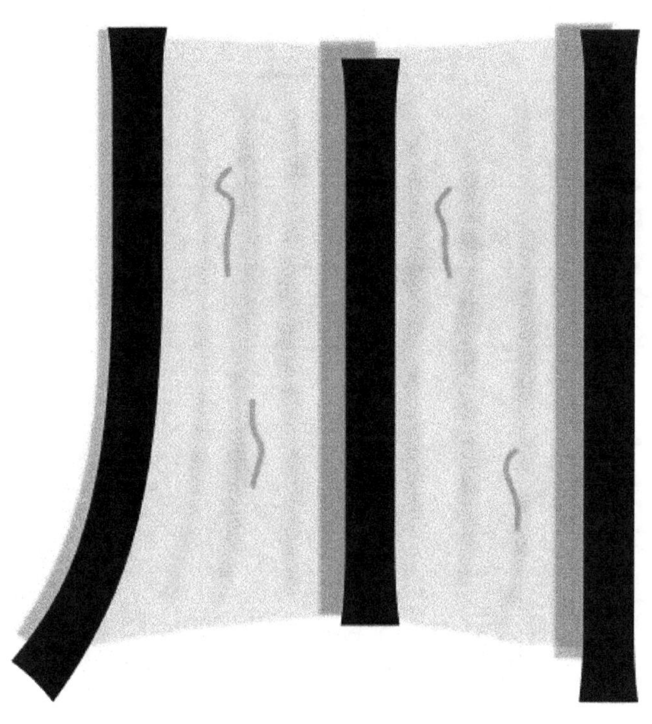

川 RIVER

"The river (川) flows between three banks"

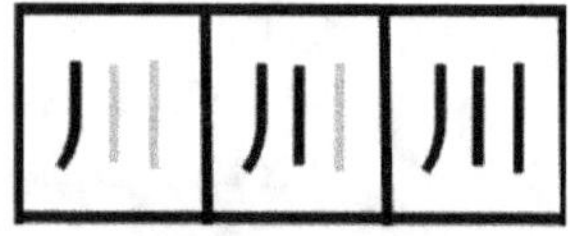

Try it:

Kun (かわ)		
かわ 川 : River		

天 HEAVEN

"Opening your arms to heaven (天)"

天 天 天 天

Try it:

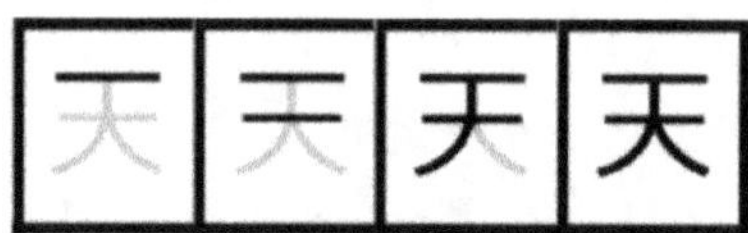

		ON (テン)		

てんき
天気: Weather

てんこう
天 候: Weather

空 SKY, EMPTY

"The cloudy sky (空) over the empty construction site"

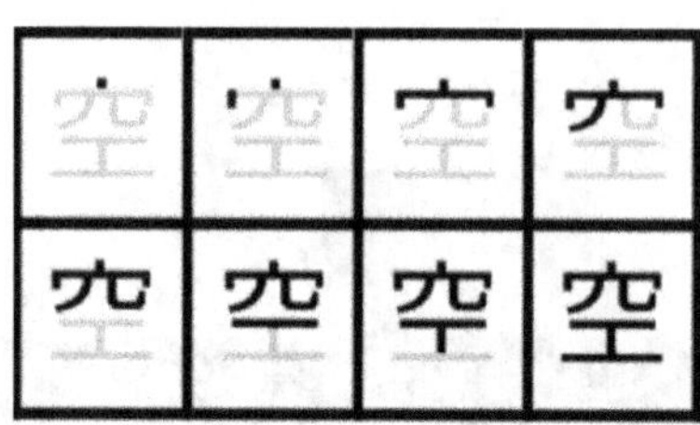

Try it:

ON (クウ)
くうき 空気: Air, atmosphere

Kun (そら, あ)
そら 空 : Sky
あ 空く : To open, to become empty

雨 RAIN

"Rain (雨) falling from the sky"

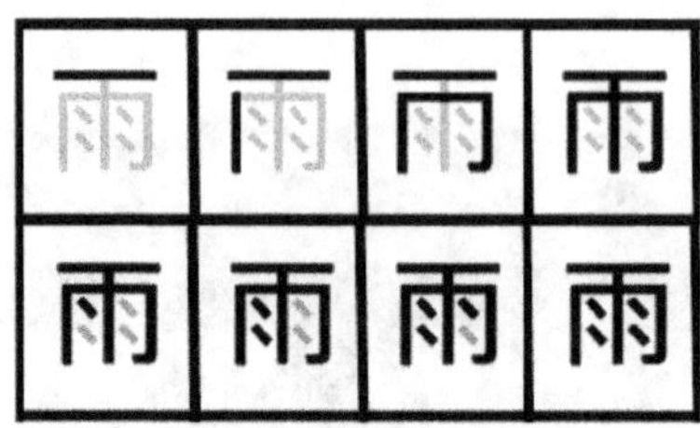

Try it:

雨	雨					

Kun (あめ)
あめ 雨 : Rain

電 ELECTRICITY

"A thunderstorm is a form of electricity (電)"

電 電 電 電 電 電 電
電 電 電 電 電 電

Try it:

電 電

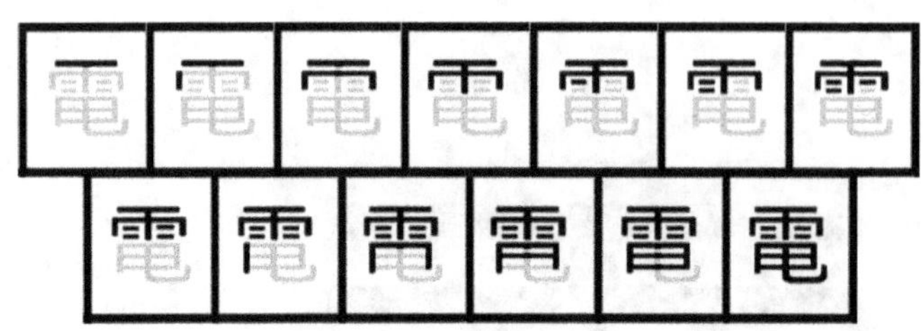

ON (デン)
でんき 電気: Electricity
でんしゃ 電 車 : Electric train
でんわ 電話: Telephone

魚 FISH

"A fish (魚) with white stripes"

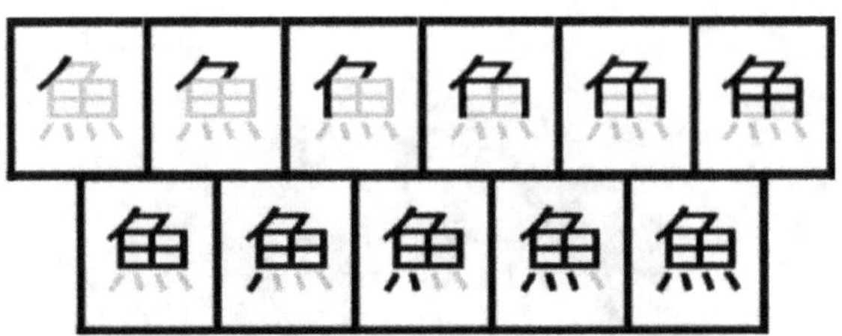

Try it:

花 FLOWER

"Two people looking at how grass (艹)
changes into flowers (花)"

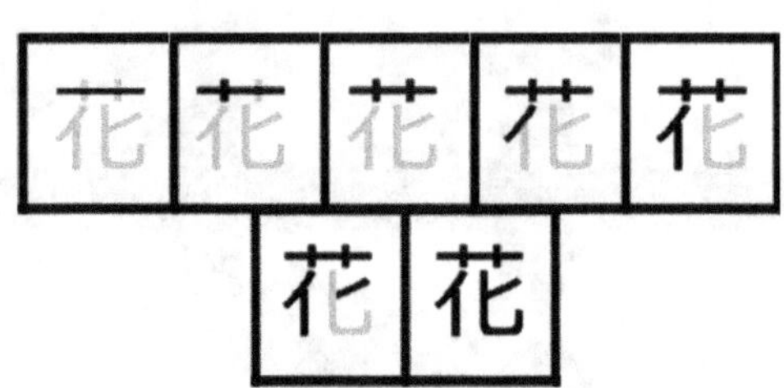

Try it:

花	花						

ON (カ)
かびん 花瓶: A vase

Kun (はな)
はな 花: Flower

気 SPIRIT, AIR

"The spirit (気) moves through the air"

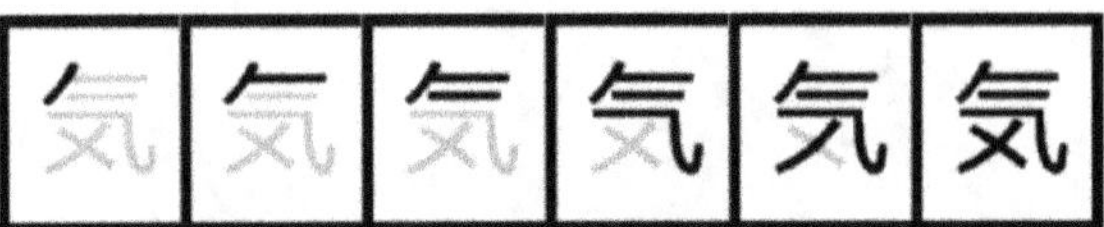

Try it:

*Note: Kanji was originally grains of rice scattered everywhere due to the wind signifying "air"

ON (キ)
げんき 元気: Health
てんき 天気: Weather
でんき 電気: Electricity
びょうき 病気: Illness
くうき 空気: Air, atmosphere

国 COUNTRY

"The king rules over the country (国)"

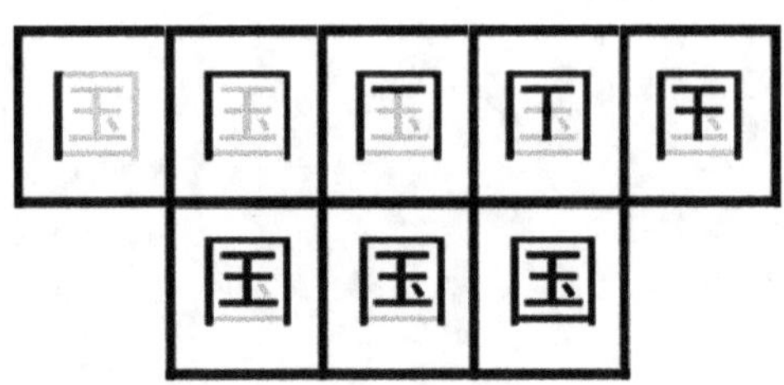

Try it:

ON (コク)
がいこく 外 国 : Foreign country
がいこくじん 外 国 人 : Foreigner

Kun (くに)
くに 国 : Country

CHAPTER 2: PEOPLE

人	友	女	男
19	20	21	22
父	母	子	
23	24	25	

人 HUMAN

"A human (人) being with long legs"

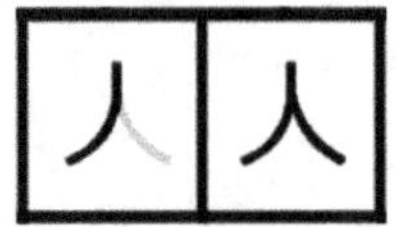

Try it:

ON (ジン, ニン)
がいこくじん 外 国 人 : Foreigner
にん 〜 人 : Counter for people

Kun (ひ と)
ひと 人 : Person

Reading Exceptions
おとな 大人 : Adult
ひとり 一人 : One person
ふたり 二人 : Two people

友 FRIEND

"It is time to hug a friend (友)"

友 友 友 友

Try it:

Note: This kanji is actually composed of two hands ナ + 又 giving the meaning of two people helping each other.

ON (ユウ)
しんゆう 親 友 : Best friend

Kun (とも)
ともだち 友 達 : Friend

女 WOMAN, FEMALE

"A woman (女) wearing a dress"

女 女 女

Try it:

女 女

Note: This kanji was originally a kneeling woman. Kanji changed over time.

Kun (おんな)
おんな 女 : Woman
おんな　こ 女 の子: Girl

男 MAN, MALE

"A strong male (男) working on the field"

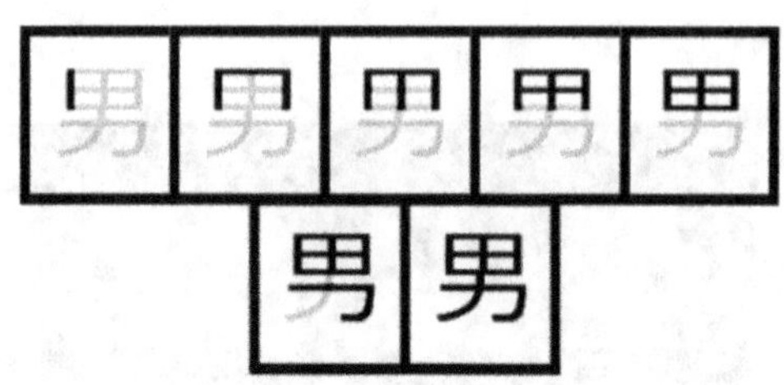

Try it:

Kun (おとこ)

おとこ
男 ：Man

おとこ　　こ
男 の子: Boy

父 FATHER

"A father (父) playing with his child"

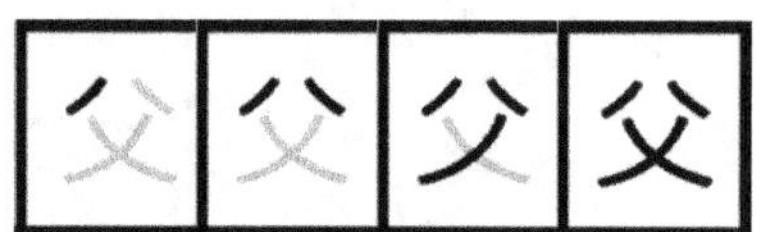

Try it:

*Note: This kanji was originally a hand holding a stone, referring to a working man.

Kun (ちち)
ちち 父 : Dad

Reading Exceptions
じ い お祖父さん : Grandfather
お じ 伯父さん : Uncle
とう お父さん : (Honorable) Father

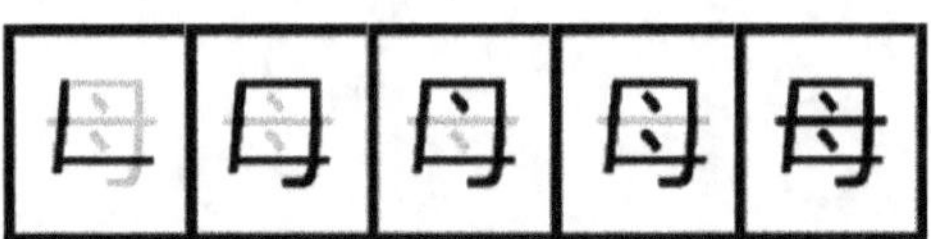 母 MOTHER

"A mother (母) hugging her child"

Try it:

*Note: This kanji was taken from a woman showing her nipples (ready to breastfeed) while kneeling.

Kun (はは)
はは 母 : Mom

Reading Exceptions
かあ お母さん: (Honorable) Mother
おば 叔母さん: Aunt

子 CHILD

"A child (子) asking for a hug"

Try it:

子	子					子

ON (シ)
お菓子 (かし): Sweets, candy
帽子 (ぼうし): Hat

Kun (こ)
男の子 (おとこ の こ): Boy
女の子 (おんな の こ): Girl
子供 (こども): Child

CHAPTER 3: BODY PARTS

目	耳	口	足	手
26	27	28	29	30

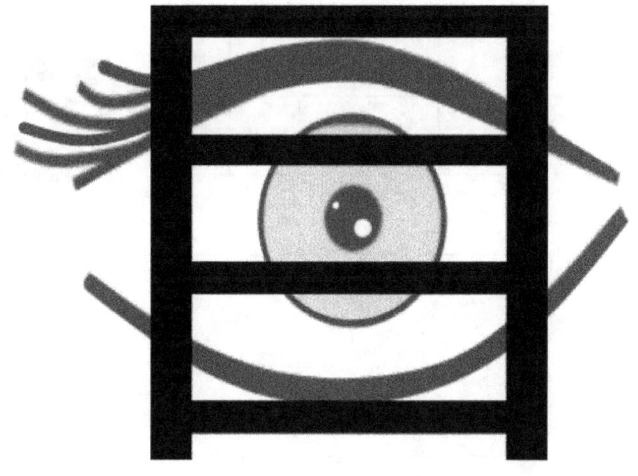

目 EYE

"A wide open eye (目)"

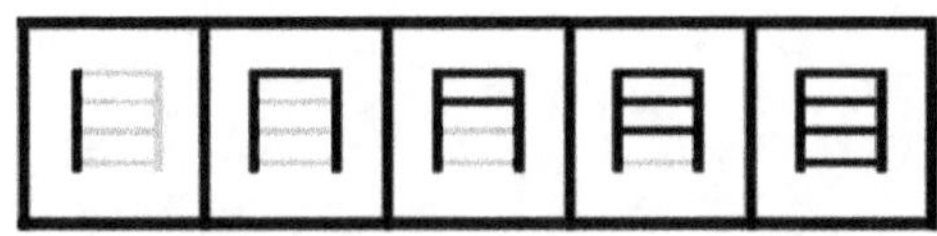

Try it:

目	目					

Kun (め)
め 目 : Eye

"A wide open eye (目)"

耳 EAR

"The folds of an ear (耳)"

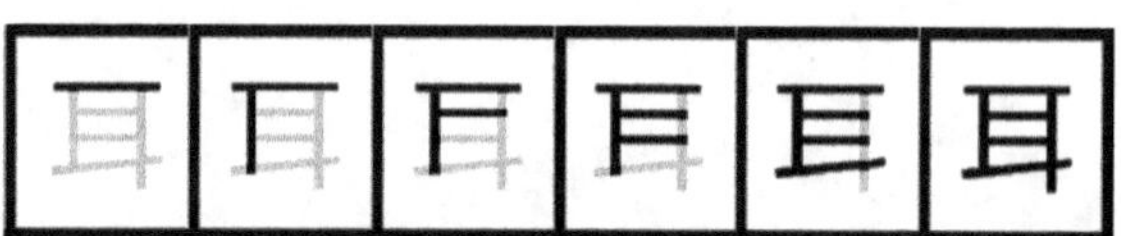

Try it:

耳	耳						

Kun (みみ)
みみ 耳 : Ear

口 MOUTH

"A wide open mouth (口)"

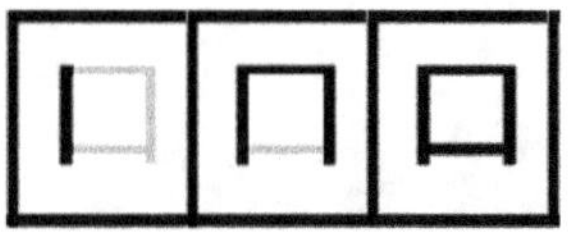

Try it:

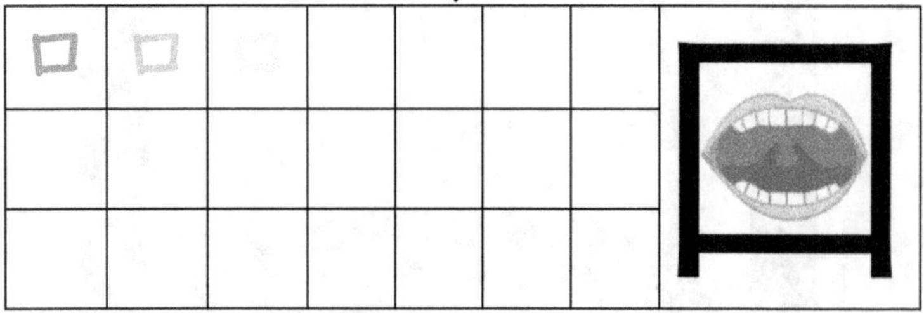

Kun (く ち)
いりぐち 入 口 : Entrance
くち 口 : Mouth
でぐち 出口 : Exit

足 LEG, ENOUGH

"Having long legs (足) is not enough to win a race"

Try it:

足	足					

Kun (あし, た)
あし 足 : Leg, foot
た 足りる : To be sufficient

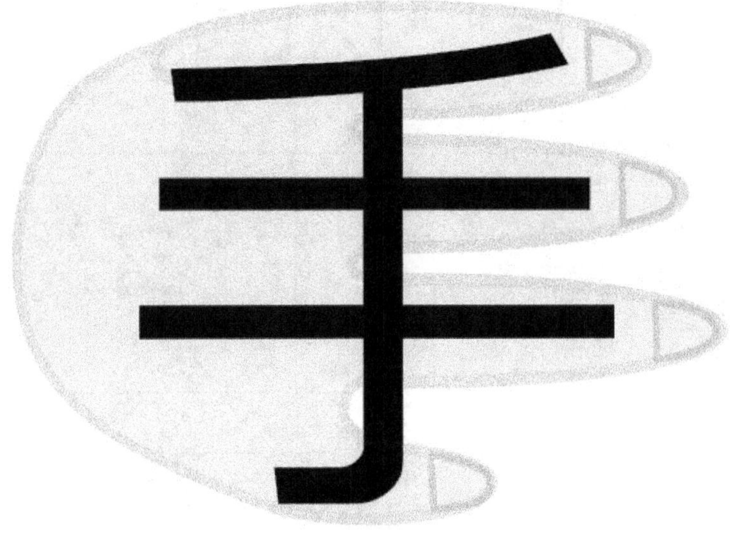

手 HAND

"A hand (手) with four fingers"

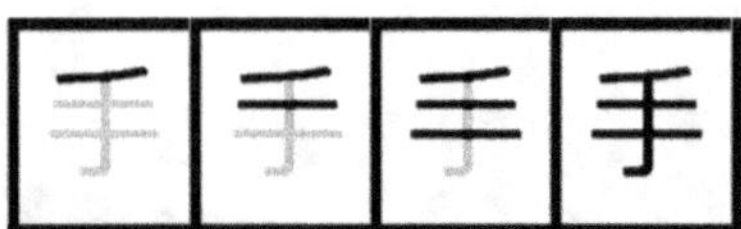

手 手 手 手

Try it:

手 手

ON (ズ)
じょうず 上手 : Skillful

Kun (て, た)
て 手: Hand
てあら お手洗い: Bathroom
きって 切手: Postage stamp
てがみ 手紙: Letter
へ た 下手: Unskillful

CHAPTER 4: SOCIETY

店	円	車	道	校
31	32	33	34	35

駅	社
36	37

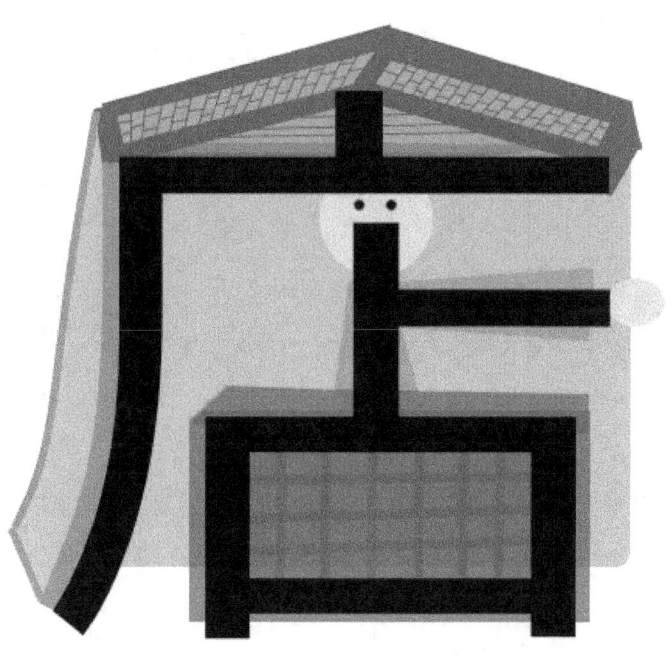

店 STORE

"An employee in the store (店)"

Try it:

ON (テン)
きっさてん 喫茶店 : Coffee lounge

Kun (みせ)
みせ 店 : Store

円 YEN, ROUND

"The yen (円) is used with both paper money and round coins"

円 円 円 円

Try it:

円 円

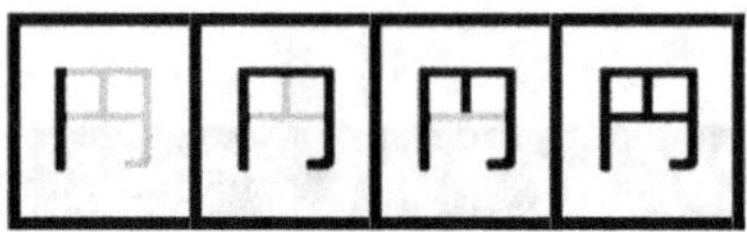

*Note: The current kanji is just a simplified version of the original.

ON (エン)
えん 〜 円 : Yen (currency)

Kun (まる)
まる 円 い: Round, circular

車 CAR

"A cart was the first idea for a car (車)"

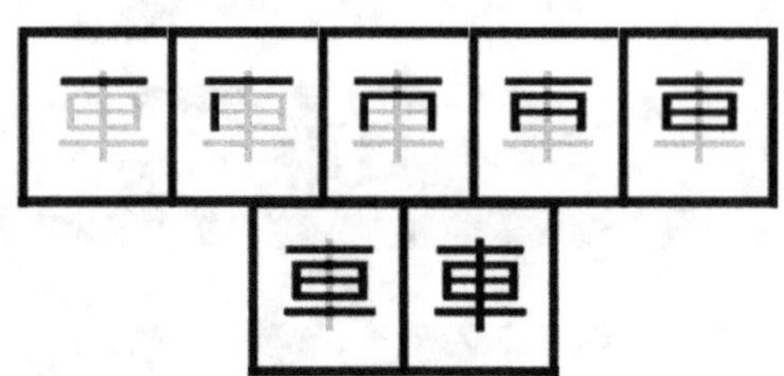

Try it:

ON (シャ)
じてんしゃ 自転車: Bicycle
じどうしゃ 自動車: Automobile
でんしゃ 電 車 : Electric train

Kun (くるま)
くるま 車 : Car

道 ROAD

"The man with the long neck (首) walks on the road (道)"

道 道 道 道 道 道
道 道 道 道 道 道

Try it:

道 道

Kun (みち)
みち 道 : Road, Street

校 SCHOOL

"The student, next to the tree (木), mingles (交) well with everyone at the school (校)"

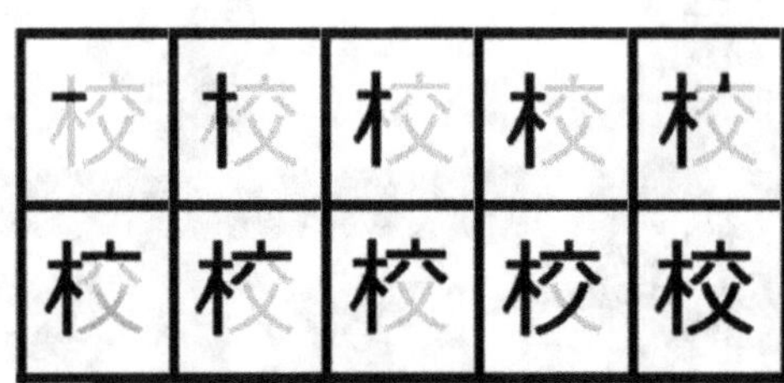

Try it:

ON (コウ)

がっこう
学 校 : School

こうこう
高 校 : High School

駅 STATION

"The horse (馬) is waiting for the train at the station (駅)"

Try it:

ON (エキ)
えき 駅 : Station

社 COMPANY

"The company (社) has a shrine (ネ) with a plant (土)"

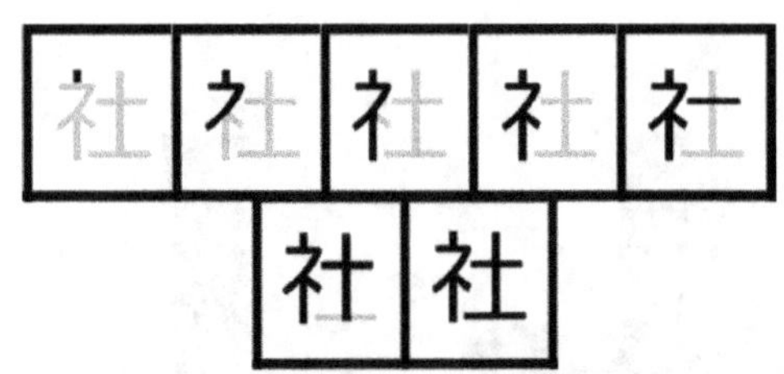

Try it:

ON (シャ)
かいしゃ 会 社 : Company
しゃかい 社 会 : Society
しゃちょう 社 長 : Company president

CHAPTER 5: ADJECTIVES

古	新	高	安	大
38	39	40	41	42
小	少	多	名	長
43	44	45	46	47
		白		
		48		

古 OLD

"An old (古) ancestral grave"

Try it:

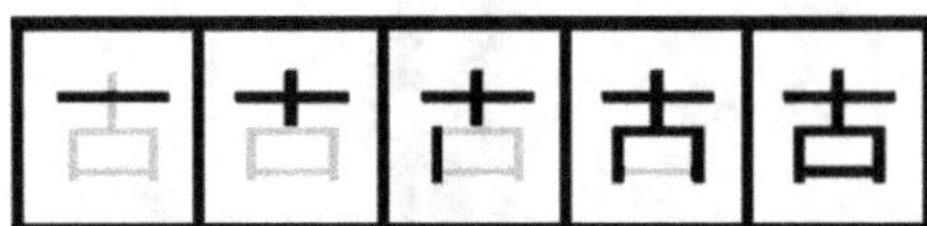

古	古					

Kun (ふる)
ふる 古 い : Old (not used for people)
ふるさと 古 里 : Home town, birthplace

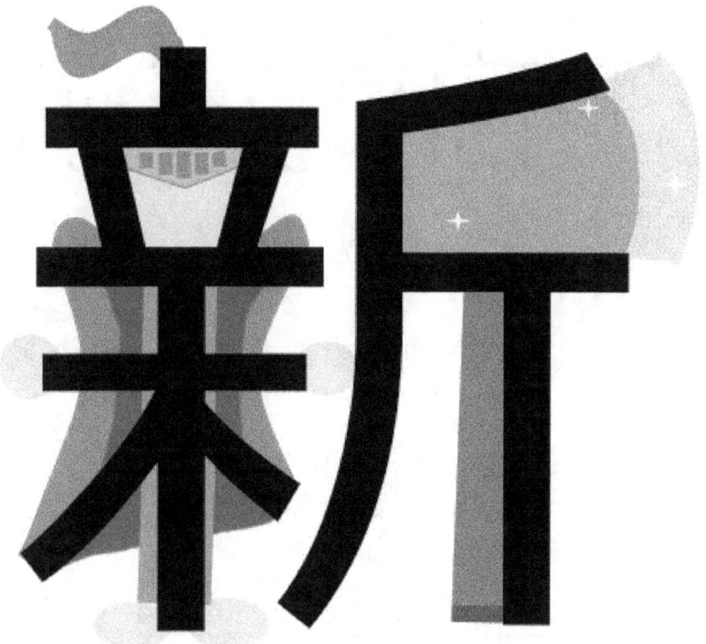

新 NEW

"A knight with a new (新) axe"

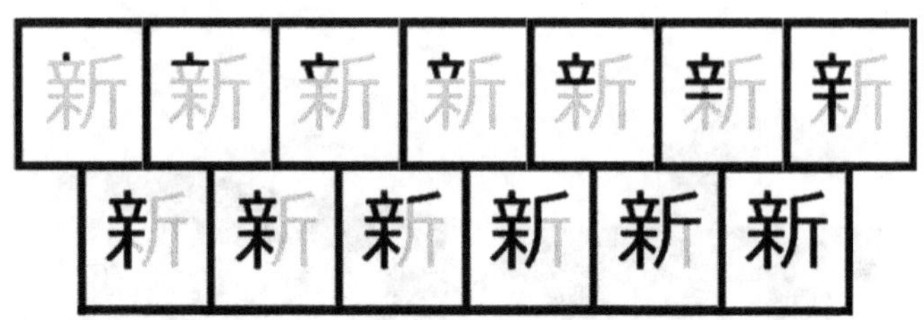

Try it:

*Note: Originally an axe to cut a tree. A freshly cut tree ended up signifying "new".

ON (シン)
しんぶん 新 聞 : Newspaper

Kun (あたら)
あたら 新 しい : New

高 TALL, EXPENSIVE

"A tall (高) and expensive building"

Try it:

高	高						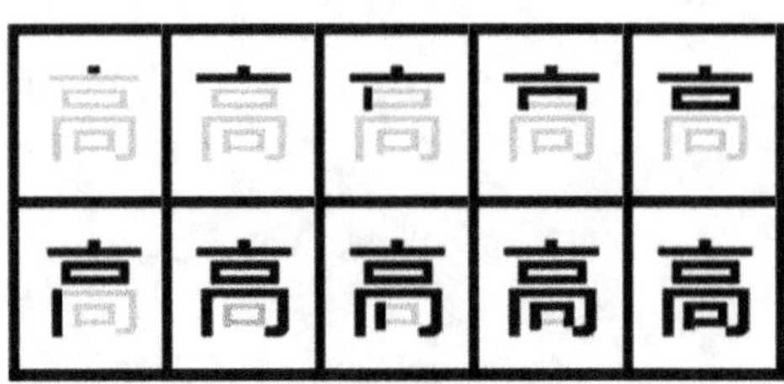

ON (コウ)
こうこう 高 校 : High School

Kun (たか)
たか 高 い : Expensive

安 CHEAP, CALM

"The calm woman paid for a cheap (安) roof"

安 安 安 安 安 安

Try it:

安 安

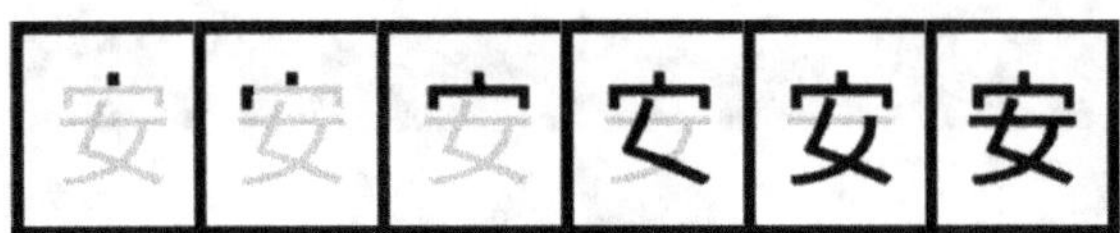

ON (アン)
あんしん 安 心 : Relief

Kun (やす)
やす 安 い : Cheap

大 BIG

"How big (大) was it? This big!"

大 | 大 | 大

Try it:

大 大

ON (ダイ, タイ)

だいがく
大 学 : University

たいしかん
大使館 : Embassy

だいじょうぶ
大 丈 夫 : All right

だいす
大好き : To be very likeable

たいせつ
大 切 : Important

Kun (おお)

おお
大 きい : (adj) Big

おお
大 きな : (n) Big

おおぜい
大 勢 : Crowd of people

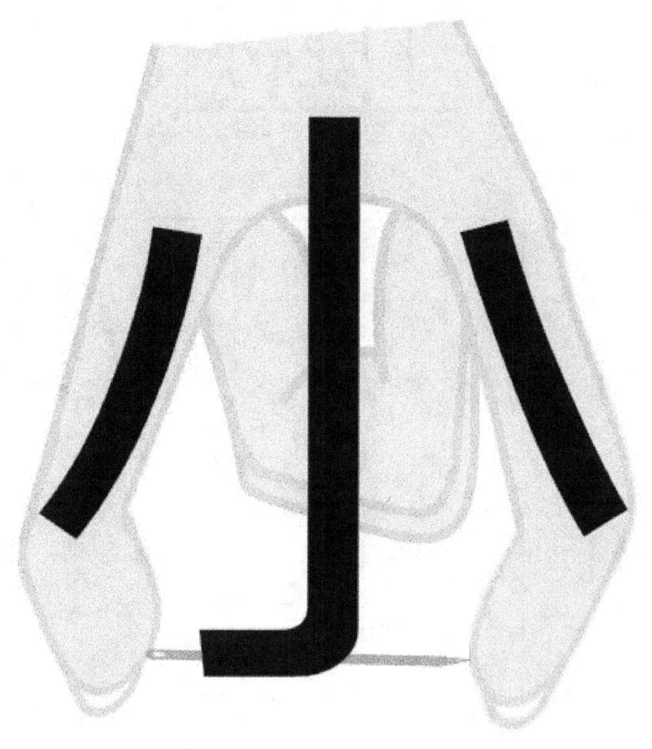

小 SMALL

"The hand is holding a small (小) needle"

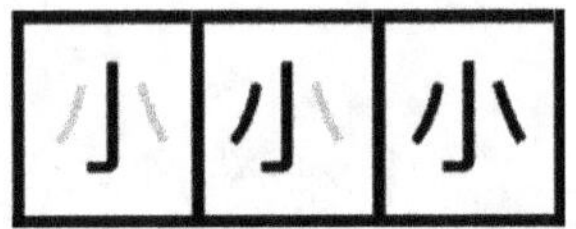

Try it:

小	小					

Kun (ちい)
ちい 小 さい: (adj) small, Little
ちい 小 さな: (n) small, Little

少 FEW

"The hand is holding a few (少) needles"

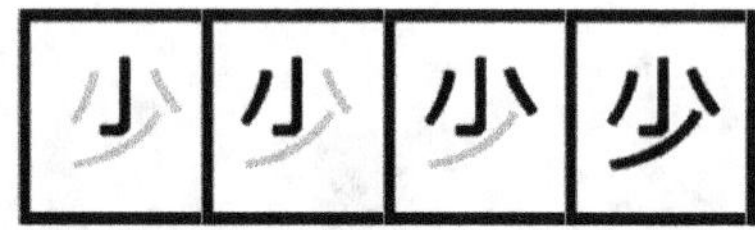

少 少 少 少

Try it:

少 少

	Kun (すく, すこ)	

すく
少 ない: A few

すこ
少 し: Few

多 MANY

"Meat was scarce in ancient times. Having two pieces of meat meant having too many (多)!"

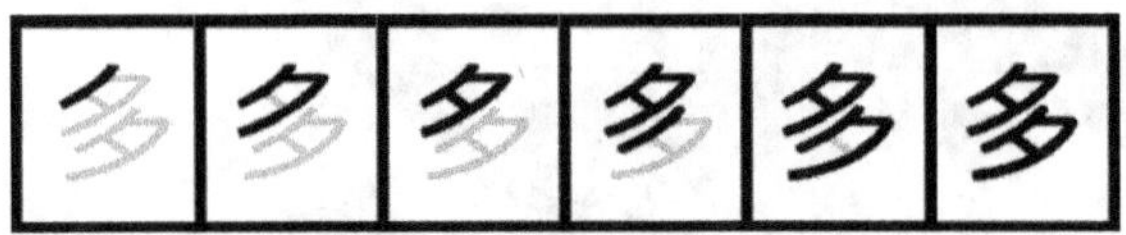

Try it:

*Note: This kanji in its current shape looks more like evening than meat. Yet, this was the original meaning.

Kun (おお)
おお 多 い : Many

名 NAME, DISTINGUISHED

"The mouth mentioned his distinguished name (名) in the evening"

名 名 名 名 名 名

Try it:

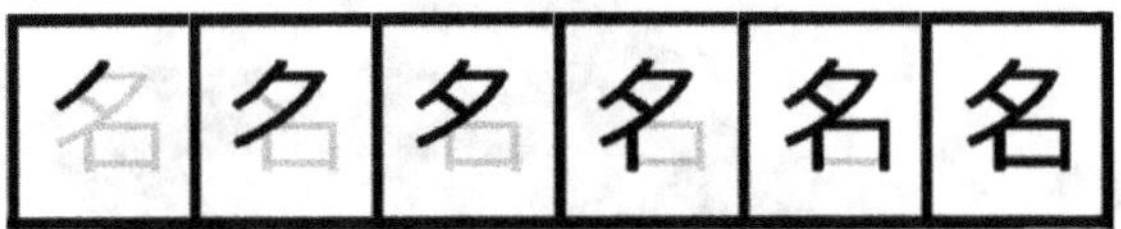

名 名

ON (メイ)

ゆうめい
有名 : Famous

Kun (な)

なまえ
名前 : Name

ひらがな
平仮名 : Hiragana

かたかな
片仮名 : Katakana

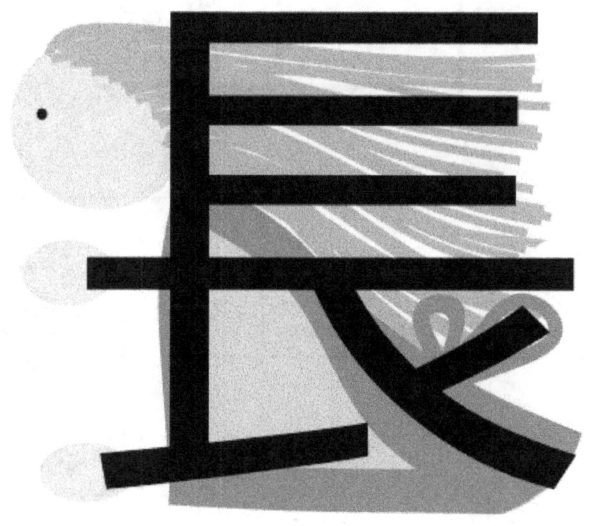

長 LONG, LEADER

"The princess with the long (長) hair is the leader"

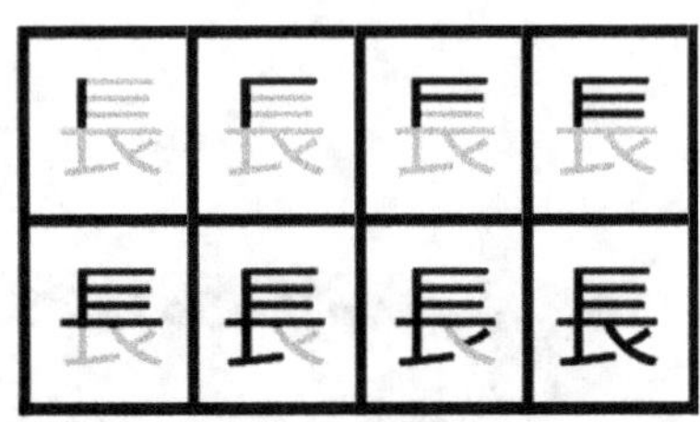

Try it:

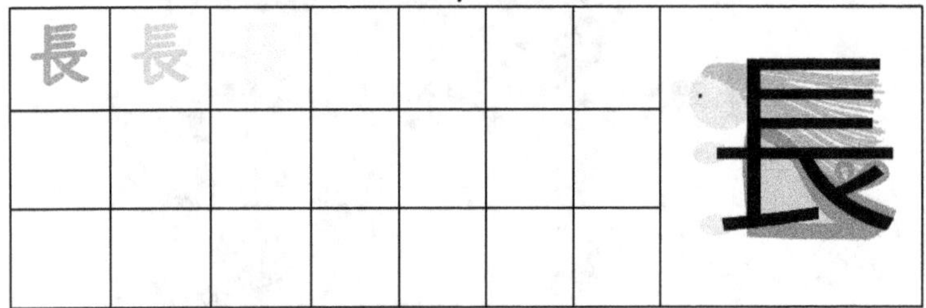

ON (チョウ)
しゃちょう 社 長 : Company president

Kun (なが)
なが 長 い: Long

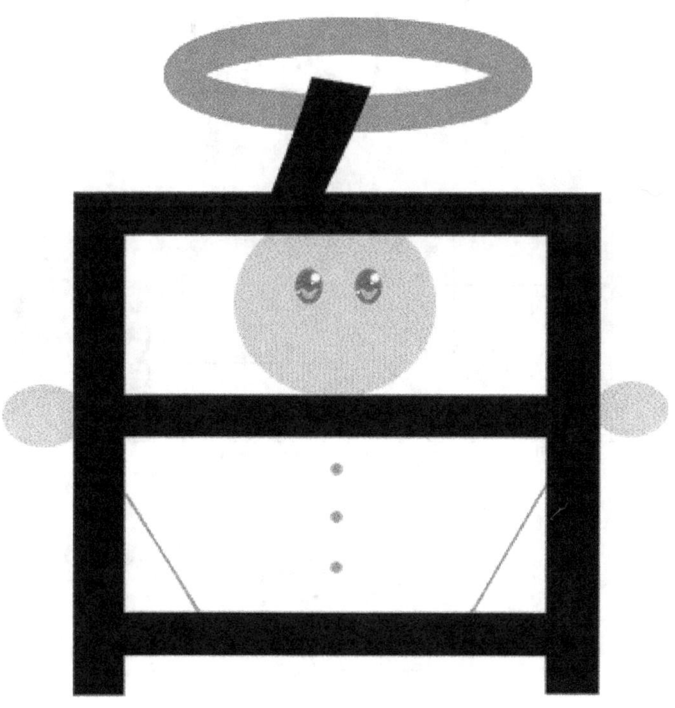

白 WHITE

"An angel with a white (白) robe"

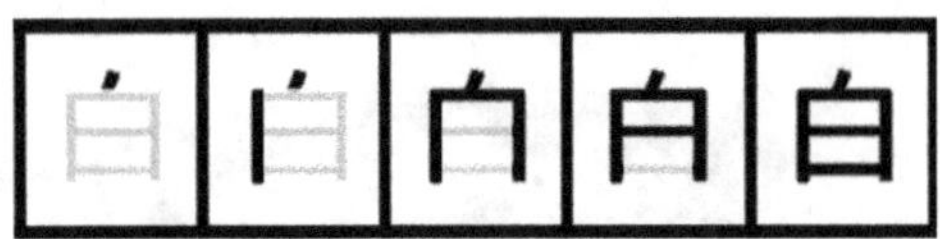

Try it:

*Note: There are multiple theories for the origin of this kanji, but not a specific one.

Kun (しろ)
しろ 白 い : (adj) White
しろ 白 : (n) White

CHAPTER 6: DIRECTION

上	下	中	外	右
49	50	51	52	53
左	後	前	北	南
54	55	56	57	58
西	東	先		
59	60	61		

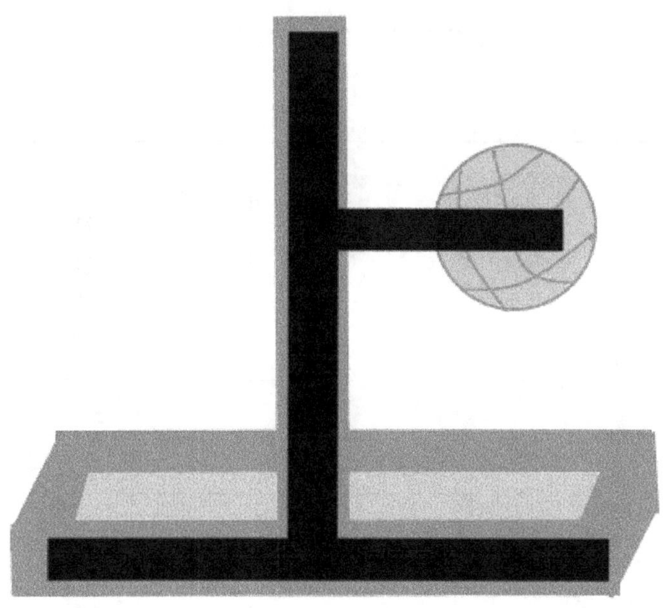

上 ABOVE

"The ball is just above (上) the volleyball court floor"

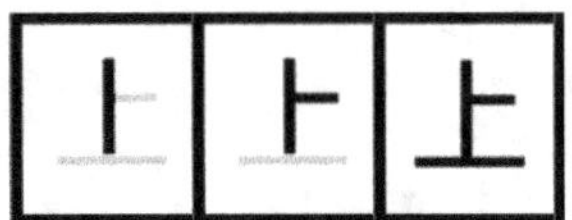

Try it:

上	上					

ON (ジョウ)
じょうず 上手 : Skillful

Kun (うえ, うわ, あ)
うえ 上 : On top of
うわぎ 上着 : Jacket
あ 上げる : To raise, to give

下 UNDER

"The treasure is buried under (下) the ground"

Try it:

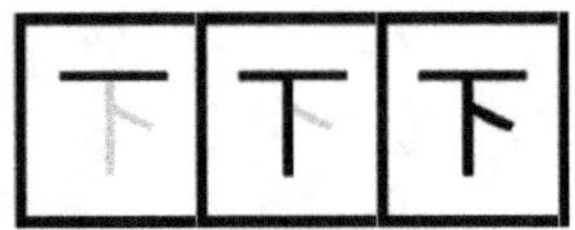

ON (カ)

ちかてつ
地下鉄: Underground train

ろうか
廊下: Corridor

Kun (した)

した
下 : Below

くつした
靴 下 : Socks

Reading Exception

へ た
下手: Unskillful

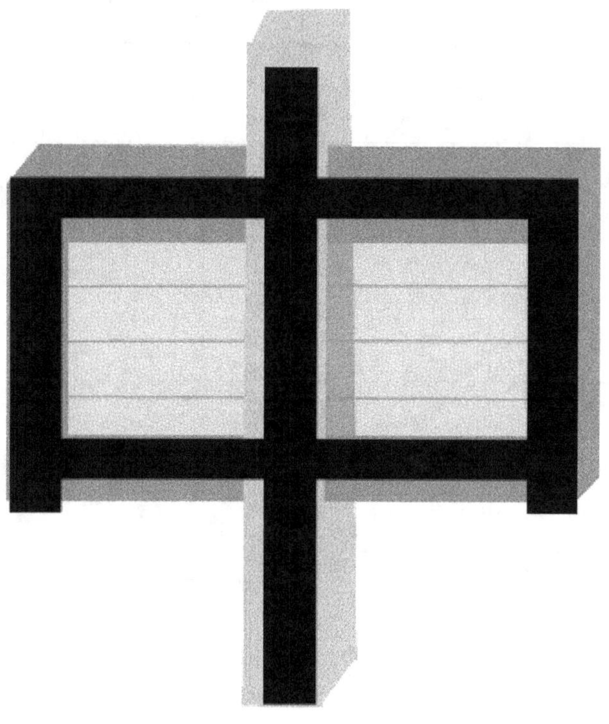

中 MIDDLE, INSIDE

"The post is inside in the middle (中) of the swinging door"

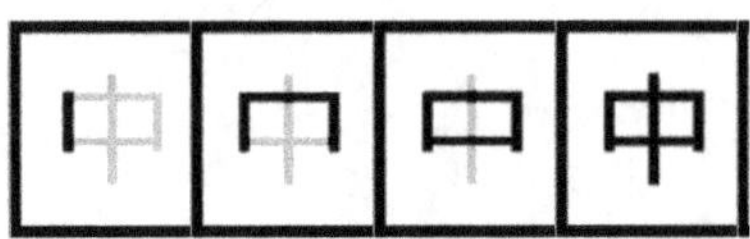

Try it:

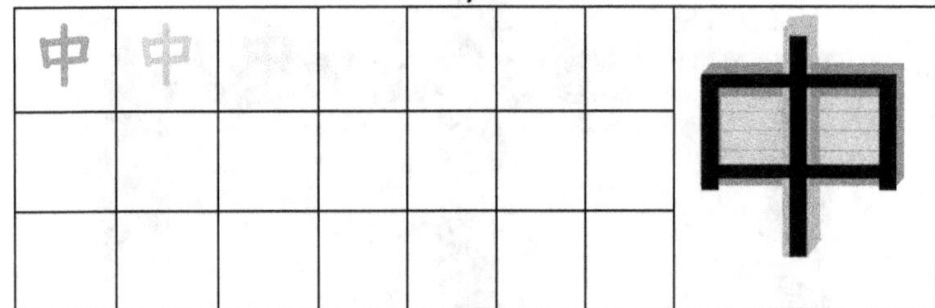

ON (チュウ)
ちゅう 〜 中 : During, while

Kun (なか)
なか 中 : Inside, middle

外 OUTSIDE

"In the evening, the man goes outside (外)
to stare at the moon"

Try it:

<table>
<tr><td>外</td><td>外</td><td></td><td></td><td></td><td></td><td></td><td rowspan="3">外</td></tr>
<tr><td></td><td></td><td></td><td></td><td></td><td></td><td></td></tr>
<tr><td></td><td></td><td></td><td></td><td></td><td></td><td></td></tr>
</table>

ON (ガイ)
がいこく 外 国 : Foreign country
がいこくじん 外 国 人 : Foreigner

Kun (そと)
そと 外 : Outside

右 RIGHT

"The right (右) hand takes the food to the mouth (口)"

Try it:

Kun (みぎ)
みぎ 右 : Right

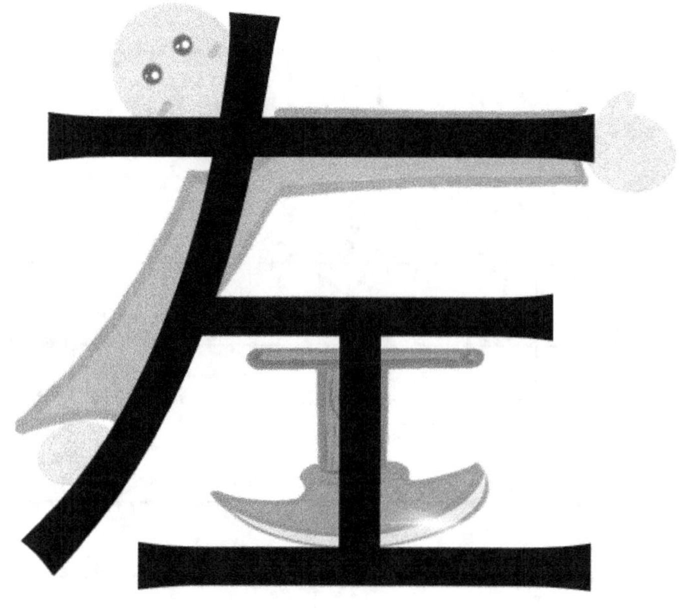

左 LEFT

"The left (左) hand holds the crafted (工) work"

左 左 左 左 左

Try it:

左 左

Kun (ひだり)
ひだり 左 : Left

後 BEHIND

"The going man (彳) gets behind (後) while taking small steps (夂) in the threaded (幺) path"

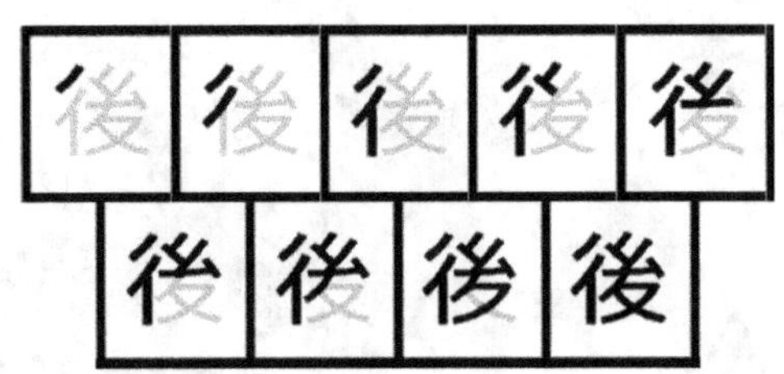

Try it:

ON (ゴ)
ご ご 午後: Afternoon (p.m.)

Kun (あと, うし)
あと 後: Afterwards
うし 後 ろ: Behind

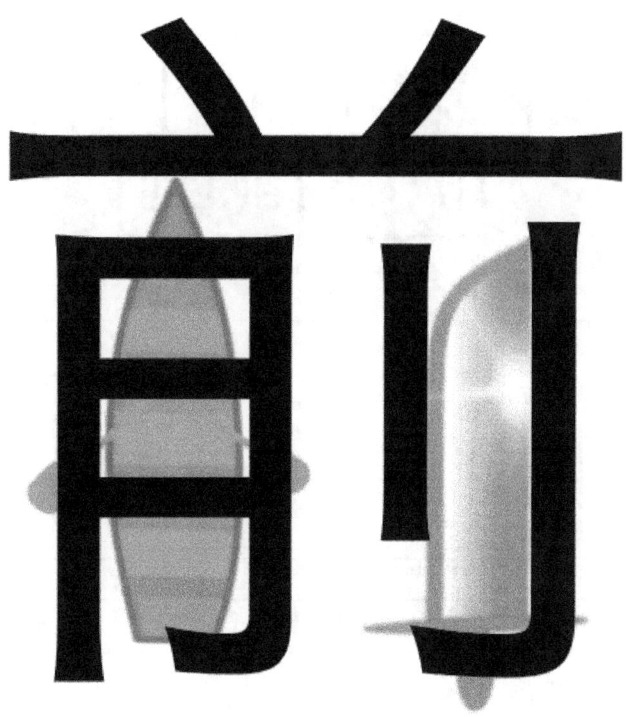

前 IN FRONT

"A way to move forward was taking a boat with a sword (刂) in front (前) for protection"

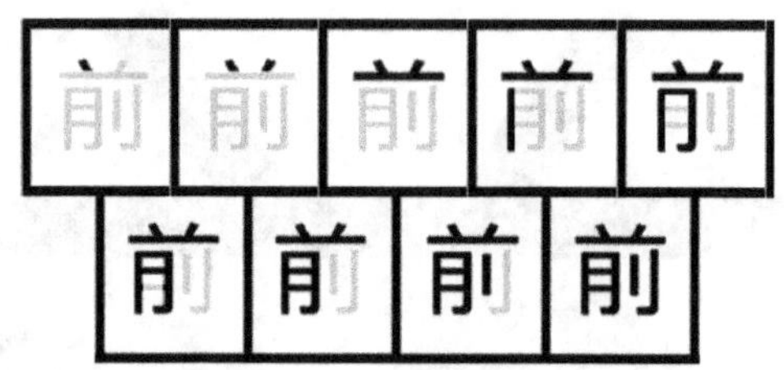

Try it:

*Note: The radical for boat and the radical for moon can sometimes be very similar.

ON (ゼン)
ごぜん 午前 : Morning (a.m.)

Kun (まえ)
まえ 前 : Before, previously
まえ 〜前 : In front of
なまえ 名前 : Name

北 NORTH

"The women, with their backs to each other, are both pointing to the north (北)"

Try it:

北	北						

Kun (き た)
き た 北 : North

南 SOUTH

"The helicopter is transporting the package to the south (南)"

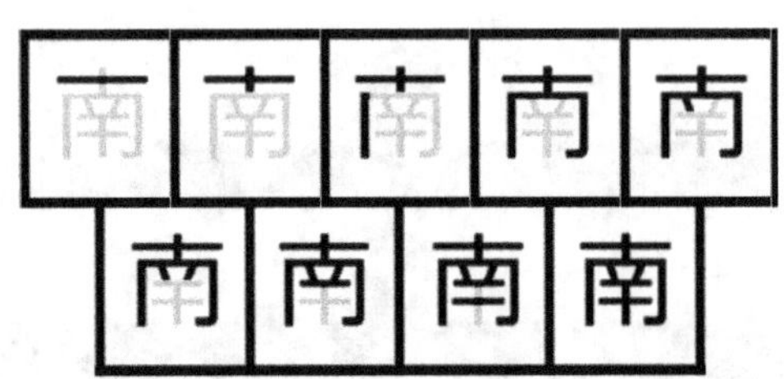

Try it:

*Note: Kanji was originally a percussion instrument hanging like a bell.

Kun (みなみ)
みなみ 南 : South

西 WEST

"A cowboy in the Old West (西)"

Try it:

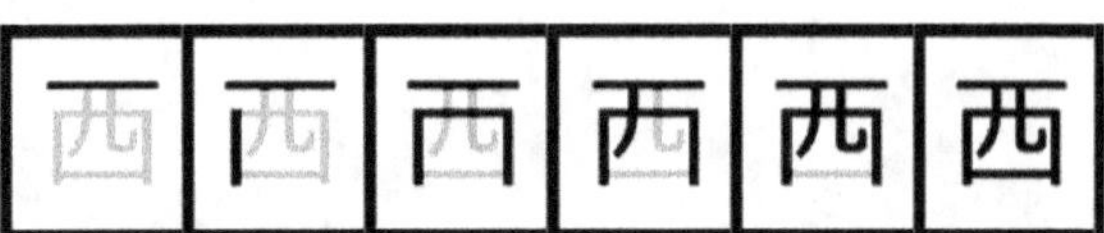

*Note: Originally a bird settling into his nest with the sun setting to the west.

Kun (にし)
にし 西 : West

東 EAST

"The sun (日) rises behind the tree (木) in the east (東)"

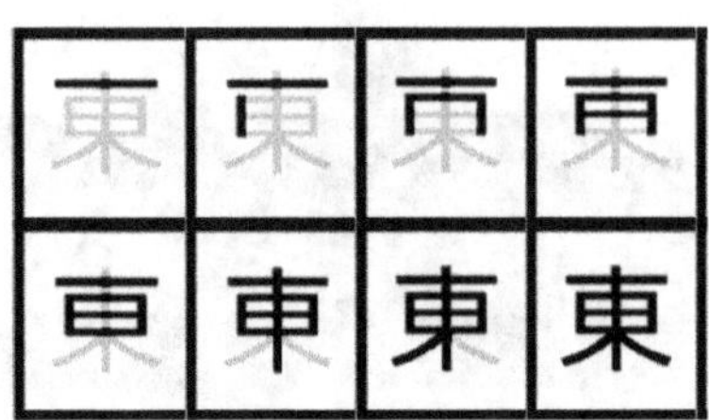

Try it:

Kun (ひがし)
ひがし 東 : East

先 FORMER, AHEAD

"The man ahead is a former (先) military officer"

先 先 先 先 先 先

Try it:

先 先

*Note: This kanji originally had a footprint on top and the legs on the bottom to give the meaning of "ahead".

ON (セン)

せんげつ
先 月 : Last month

せんしゅう
先 週 : Last week

せんせい
先 生 : Teacher, doctor

Kun (さき)

さき
先 : The future, previous

CHAPTER 7: TIME

分	半	年	午	何
62	63	64	65	66
每	時	間	今	週
67	68	69	70	71

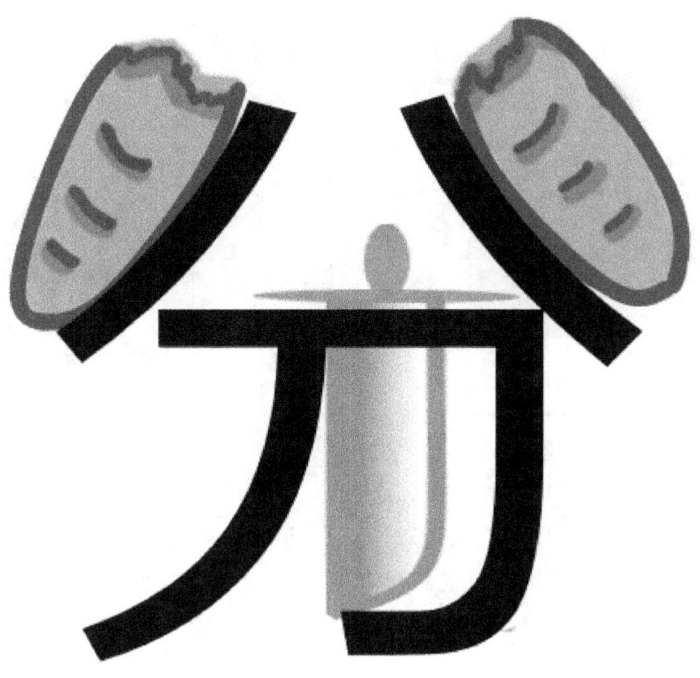

分 SHARE, MINUTE

"It took one minute (分) to cut the bread so we could share it"

分 分 分 分

Try it:

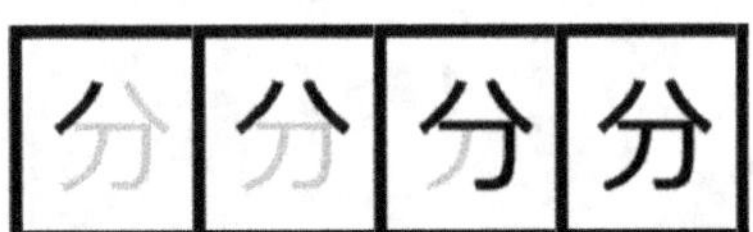

ON (ブン)
じぶん 自分: Oneself
はんぶん 半分: Half
ぶん 〜分: 〜Minutes

Kun (わ)
わ 分かる: To understand

半 HALF

"The ruler measures the logs to be cut in half (半)"

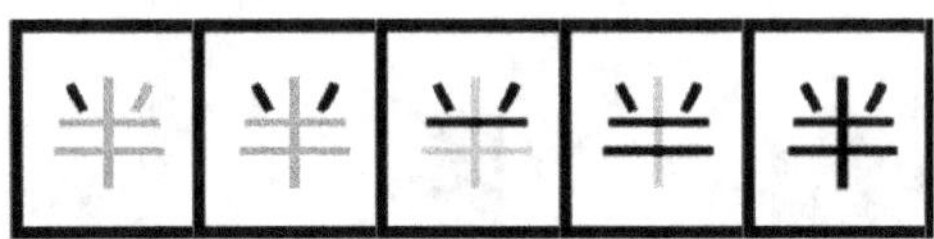

Try it:

半	半						

ON (ハン)
はん 半 : Half
はんぶん 半 分 : Half

年 YEAR

"A cycle of rice crops harvest is every year (年)"

年 年 年 年 年 年

Try it:

年	年				

ON (ネン)

きょねん
去 年 : Last year

らいねん
さ 来 年 : Year after next

まいねん
毎 年 : Every year

まんねんひつ
万 年 筆 : Fountain pen

らいねん
来 年 : Next year

Kun (とし)

とし
年 : Year

おととし
一昨年 : Year before last

ことし
今年 : This year

まいとし
毎 年 : Every year

午 NOON

"Twelve fingers to represent noon (午)"

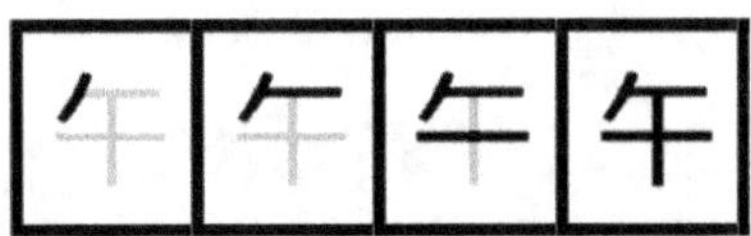

Try it:

ON (ゴ)
ご ご 午後: Afternoon (p.m.)
ごぜん 午前: Morning (a.m.)

"Twelve fingers to represent noon (午)"

何 WHAT

"A confused person (亻) opens the mouth (口) and asks: What (何)?"

何 何 何 何 何 何 何

Try it:

Kun (なに, なん)
なに 何 : What
なん 何 : What
なん 何 〜 : What sort of 〜

毎 EVERY

"Every father and every (毎) mother (母) has a child"

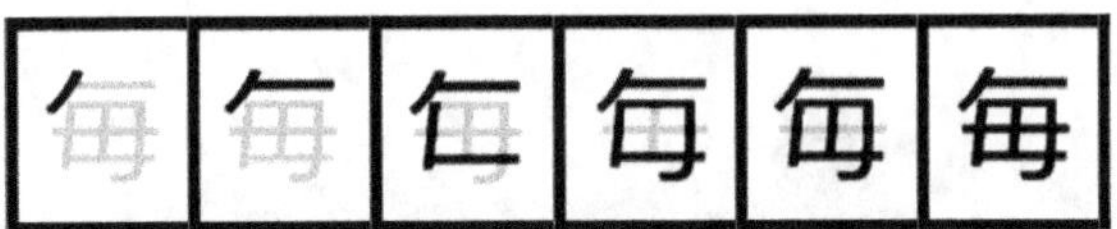

Try it:

ON (マイ)

まいあさ
毎 朝 : Every morning

まいげつ
毎 月 : Every month

まいしゅう
毎 週 : Every week

まいにち
毎 日 : Every day

まいとし
毎 年 : Every year

まいばん
毎 晩 : Every night

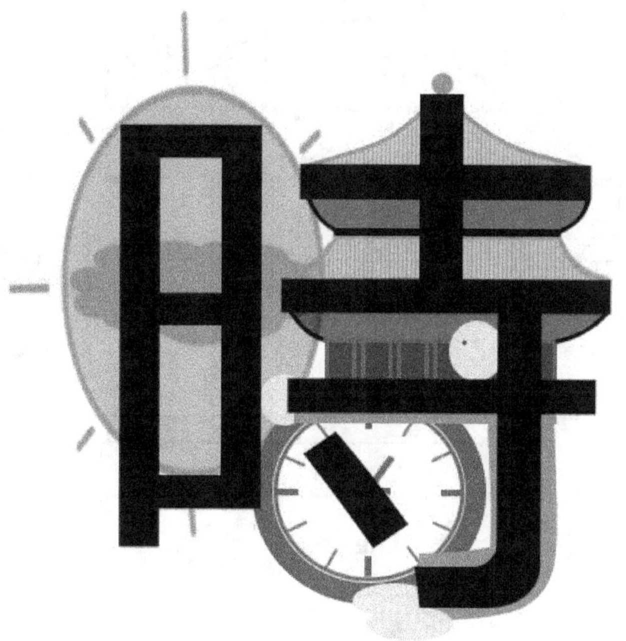

時 TIME

"The sun (日) helps to measure time (時) at the temple (寺)"

Try it:

ON (ジ)
じ 〜時: Time (〜O'clock) じかん 時間: Time

Kun (とき)
とき 〜時 : At the time of 〜 ときどき 時 々 : Sometimes

Reading Exception
とけい 時計: Watch, clock

間 BETWEEN

"The sun (日) is in between (間) the two doors"

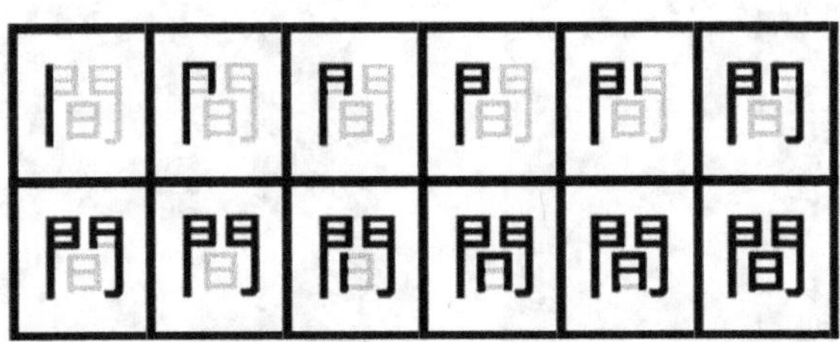

Try it:

ON (カン)
じかん 時間: Time
じかん 〜時間: 〜Hours
しゅうかん 〜週間: 〜Weeks

今 NOW

"The cuckoo clock sings now (今)"

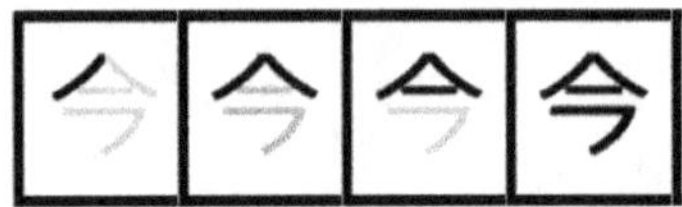

Try it:

*Note: This kanji was originally the cover of a bottle.

ON (コン)
こんげつ 今 月 : This month
こんしゅう 今 週 : This week
こんばん 今 晩 : This evening

Kun (いま)
いま 今 : Now

Reading Exceptions
きょう 今日 : Today
け さ 今朝 : This morning
ことし 今年 : This year

週 WEEK

"Each week (週) I walk down the road (辶)
to see the plant (土) grow"

週 週 週 週 週 週
週 週 週 週 週

Try it:

週 週

ON (シュウ)

こんしゅう
今 週 : This week

せんしゅう
先 週 : Last week

まいしゅう
毎 週 : Every week

らいしゅう
来 週 : Next week

しゅうかん
〜 週 間 : 〜Weeks

CHAPTER 8: NUMBERS

一	二	三	四	五
72	73	74	75	76
六	七	八	九	十
77	78	79	80	81
百	千	万		
82	83	84		

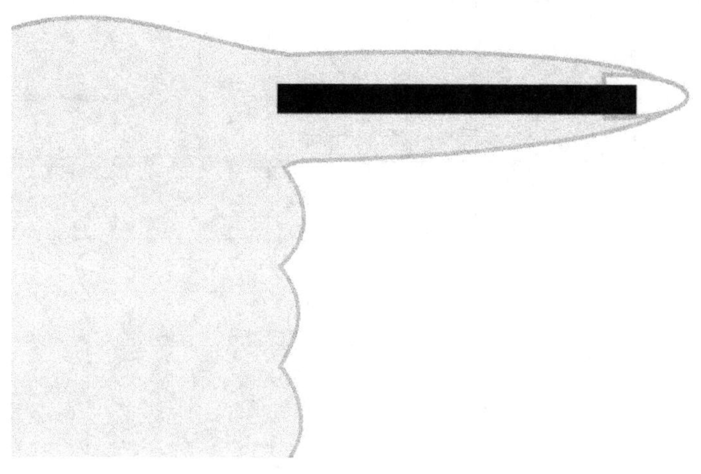

一 ONE

"One (一) finger"

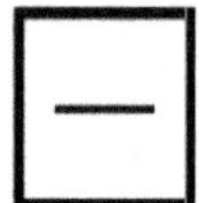

Try it:

ON (イ チ)

いち
一 : One

いちにち
一 日 : One day, Whole day

ついたち
一 日 : First day of month

いっしょ
一 緒 : Together

Kun (ひ と)

ひと
一 つ : One

ひとつき
一 月 : One month

ひとり
一 人 : One person

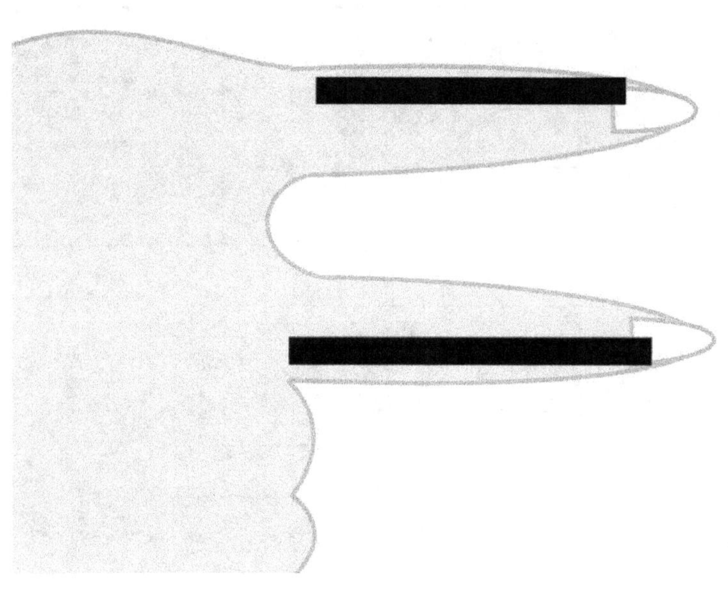

二 TWO

"Two (二) fingers"

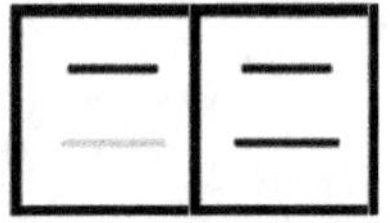

Try it:

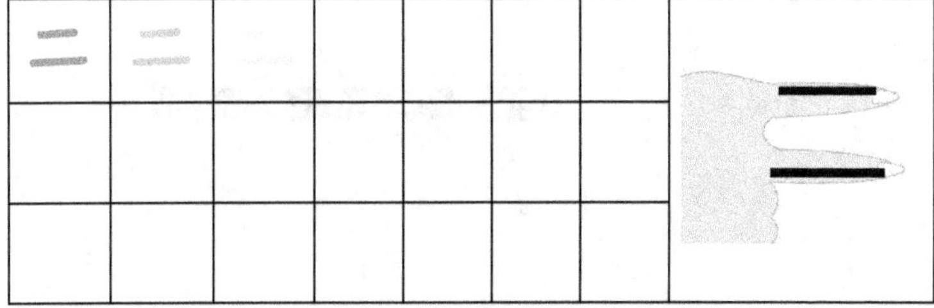

ON (二)

に
二: Two

Kun (ふた)

ふたり
二人: Two people

Reading Exceptions

はたち
二十歳: 20 years old

はつか
二十日: Twenty days, twentieth

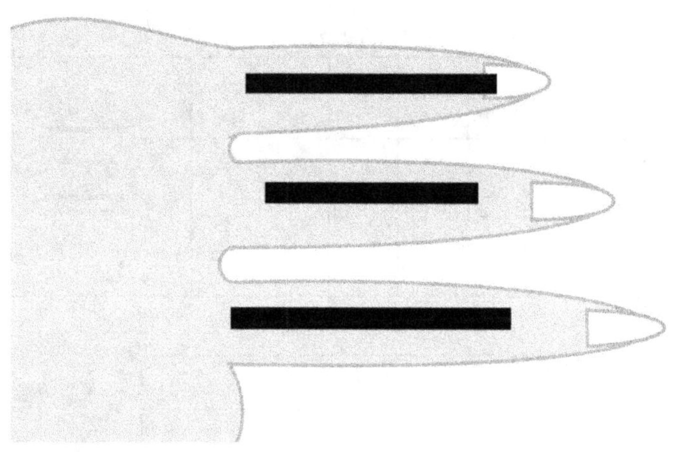

三 THREE

"Three (三) fingers"

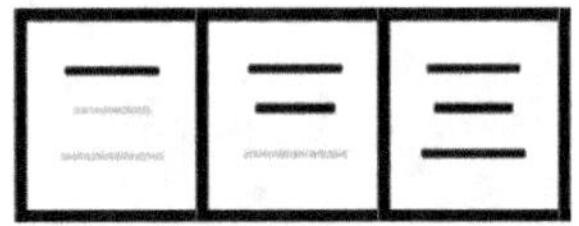

Try it:

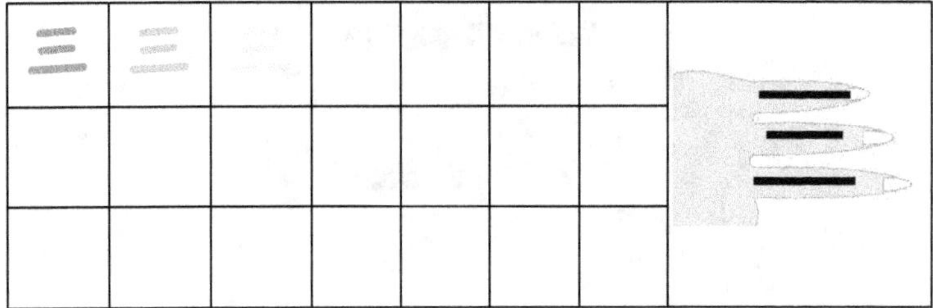

ON (サン)

さん
三 : Three

Kun (み, みっ)

みっか
三日: Three days, third day of the month

みっ
三つ: Three

四 FOUR

"Four (四) fingers framing two legs (儿)"

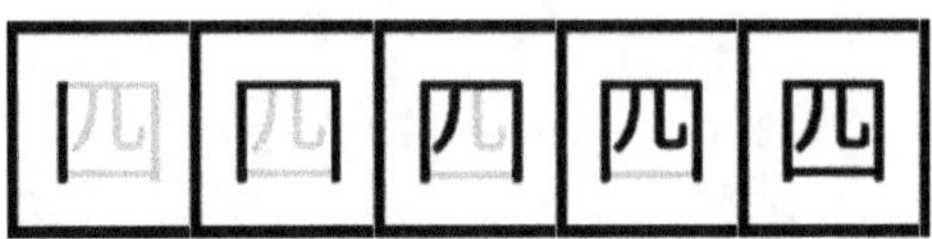

Try it:

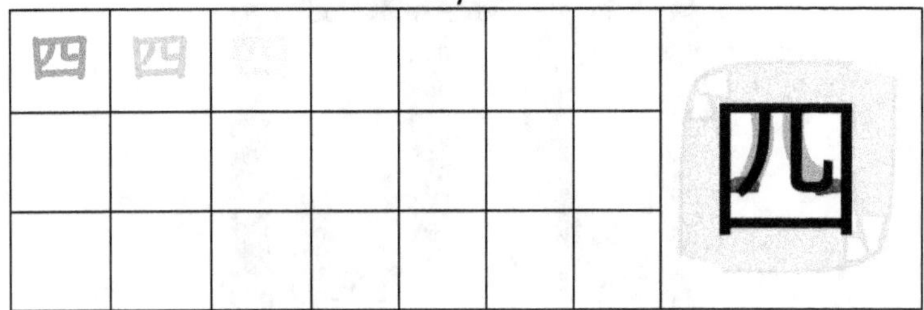

ON (シ)
し 四: Four

Kun (よん, よっ)
よん 四 : Four
よっか 四日: Four days, Fourth day of the month
よっ 四 つ: Four

五 FIVE

"It is just the number five (五)"

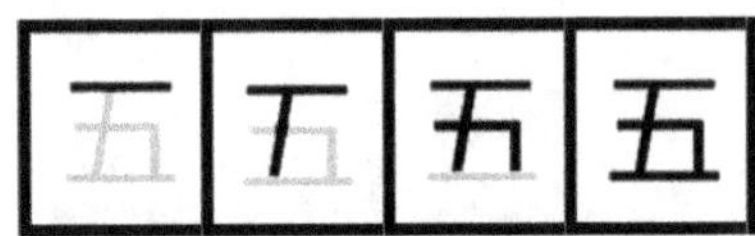

Try it:

							五
五	五						

ON (ゴ)
ご 五: Five

Kun (いつ)
いつか 五日: Five days, fifth day いつ 五つ: Five

六 SIX

"Five fingers and a thumb equal six (六)"

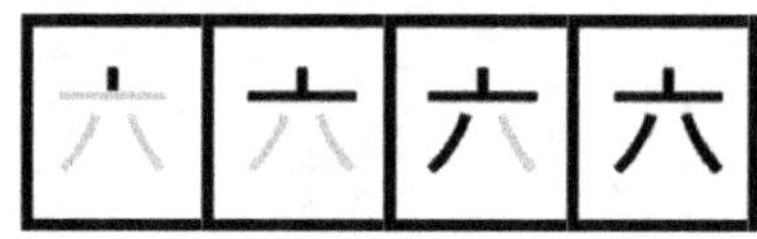

Try it:

ON (ロク)
ろく 六 : Six

Kun (む, むっ, むい)
むいか 六日 : Six days, sixth day of the month むっ 六つ : Six

七 SEVEN

"An upside down number seven (七)"

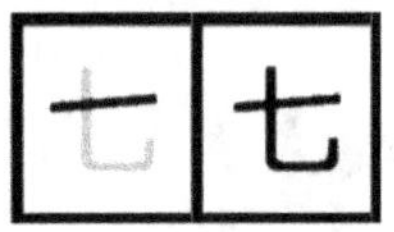

Try it:

*Note: The kanji for 7 used to have a different meaning, then it was borrowed to mean 7.

ON (シチ)
しち 七 : Seven

Kun (なな, なの)
なな 七 : Seven
なな 七つ : Seven
なのか 七日 : Seven days, seventh day

八 EIGHT

"An eight (八) without the twist"

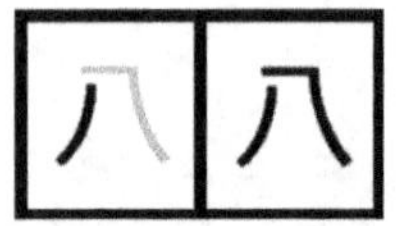

Try it:

八	八						

*Note: This kanji looks like it was split into two, that's because 8 is a multiple of two.

ON (ハチ)
はち 八 : Eight

Kun (や, やっ, よう)
やおや 八百屋: Greengrocer
やっ 八 つ: Eight
ようか 八 日: Eight days, eighth day of the month

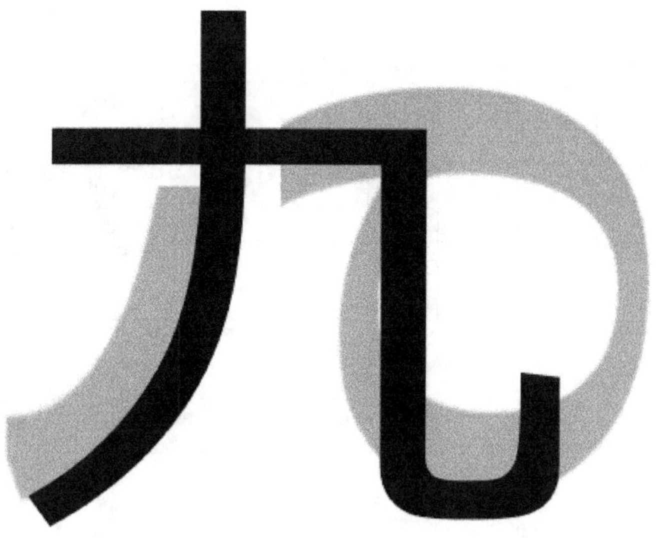

九 NINE

"A broken nine (九)"

Try it:

*Note: This kanji was originally a broken elbow with fingers, signifying something that was almost complete, but fell short.

ON (キュウ, ク)
きゅう 九 : Nine
く 九: Nine

Kun (ここの)
ここのか 九 日 : Nine days, ninth day
ここの 九 つ: Nine

 十 TEN

"A person showing all ten (十) fingers"

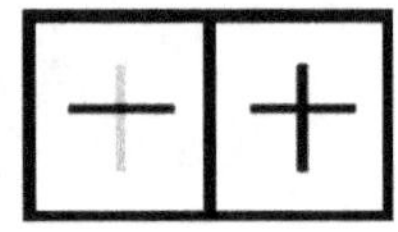

Try it:

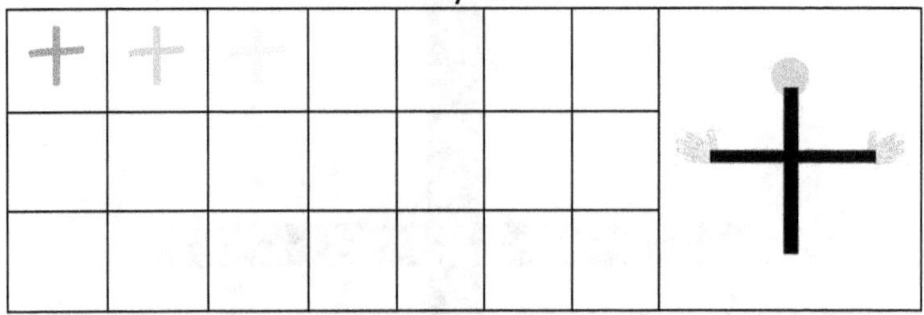

*Note: Before becoming a cross, this kanji just had a large dot in the middle, to signify a bundle of ten.

ON (ジュウ)
じゅう 十 : Ten

Kun (とお)
とお 十 : Ten
とおか 十日 : Ten days, the tenth day

百 HUNDRED

"A hundred (百) turned sideways"

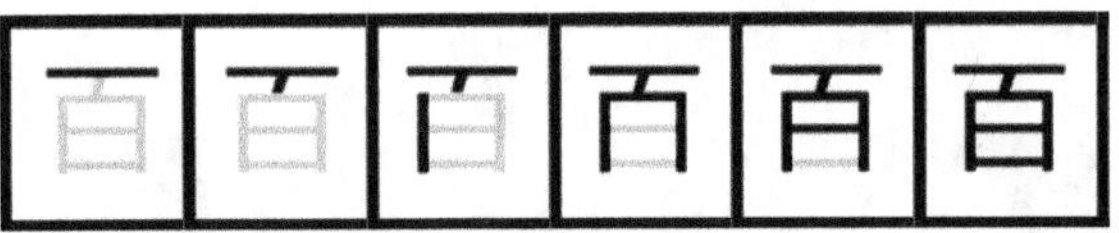

Try it:

ON (ヒャク)
ひゃく 百 : One hundred

Reading Exception
やおや 八百屋: Greengrocer

千 THOUSAND

"Three lines form the letter "t" for the word thousand (千)"

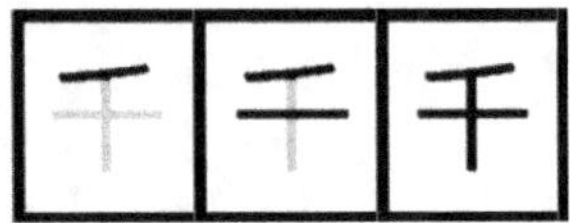

Try it:

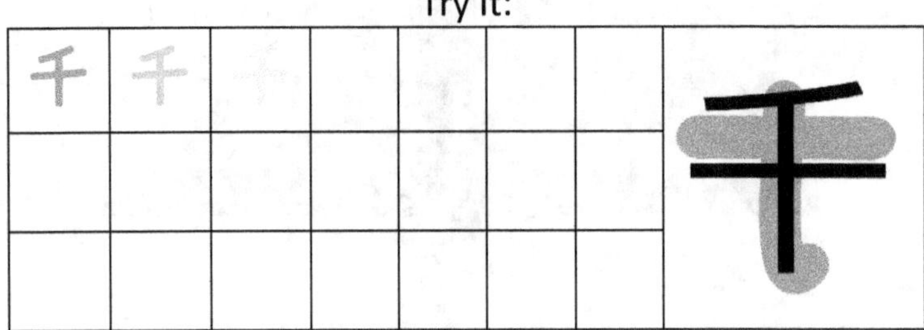

*Note: This kanji was originally a person (人) with the kanji of one (一) across to signify a number.

ON (セン)
せん 千 : Thousand

¥10,000

万 TEN THOUSAND

"A thief stole a bag of 10,000 (万) yen"

万 万 万

Try it:

万	万							

*Note: This kanji was originally a tribal name, then it was borrowed to mean ten thousand.

ON (マン)

まん
万 : Ten thousand

まんねんひつ
万 年 筆 : Fountain pen

CHAPTER 9: VERBS

行	来	入	出	言
85	86	87	88	89
語	読	書	話	聞
90	91	92	93	94
食	飲	立	休	見
95	96	97	98	99
会	学	生	買	
100	101	102	103	

行 GO

"The man is ready to go (行) on his way"

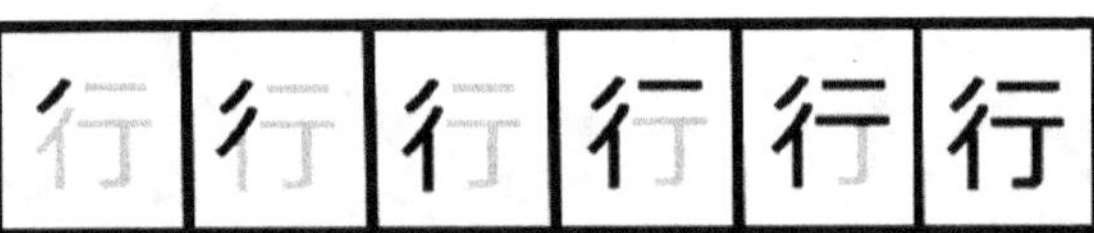

Try it:

ON (コウ)
ぎんこう 銀行 : Bank
ひこうき 飛行機 : Airplane
りょこう 旅行 : Travel

Kun (い, ゆ)
い 行く : To go
ゆ 行く : To go

来 COME

"The woman has finally come (来) to the cabin"

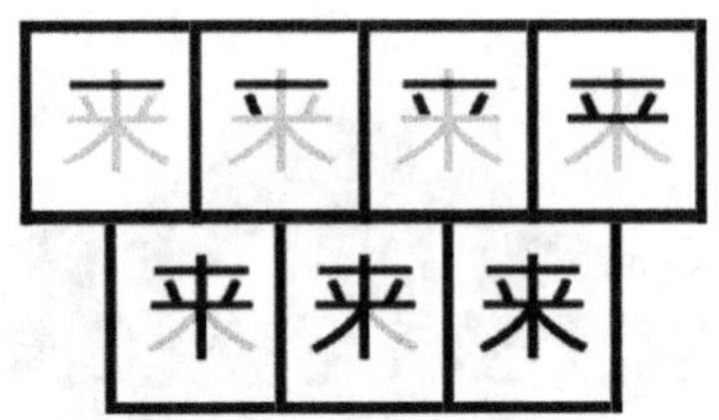

Try it:

*Note: Originally this kanji was a barley plant.

ON (ライ)
らいねん さ 来 年 : Year after next
らいげつ 来 月 : Next month
らいしゅう 来 週 : Next week
らいねん 来 年 : Next year

Kun (く)
く 来 る : To come

入 ENTER

"Enter (入) the tent"

Try it:

入	入						入

Kun (い、はい)
はい 入る: To enter い 入れる: To put in

Reading Exception
いりぐち 入口 : Entrance

出 EXIT

"I exit (出) the fortress and go to the mountains (山)"

Try it:

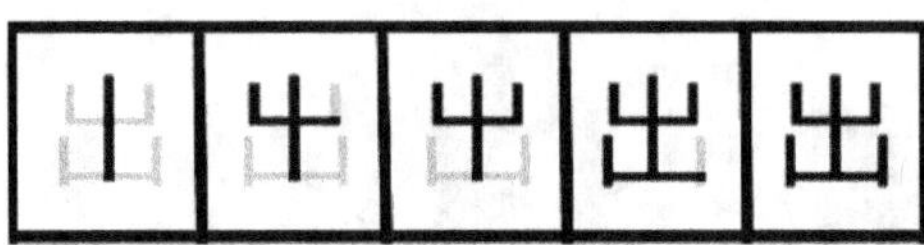

Kun (で, だ)
だ 出す: To put out
で 出かける: To go out
でぐち 出口: Exit
で 出る: To appear, to leave

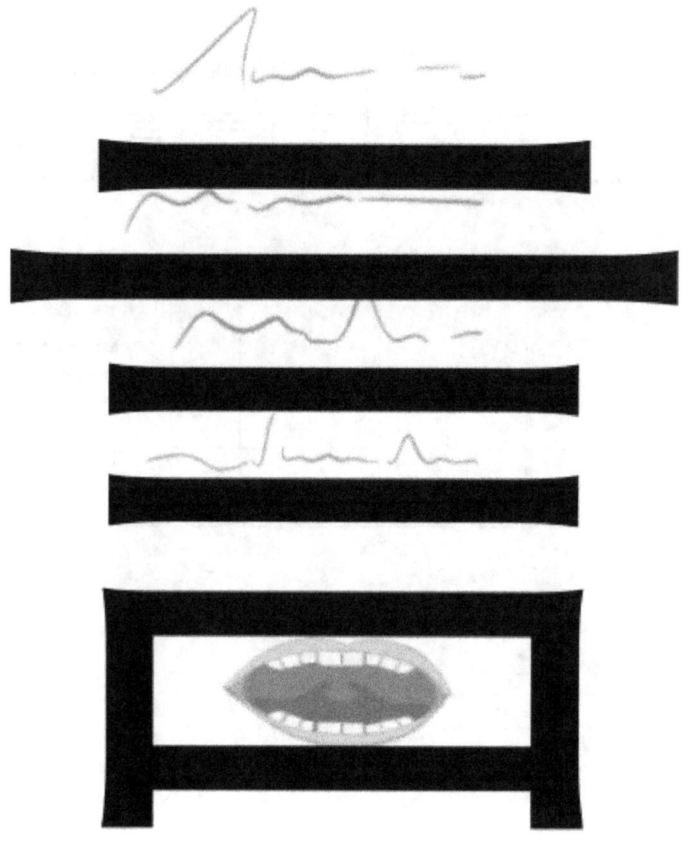

言 SAY, WORD

"The mouth (口) says (言) all kinds of words"

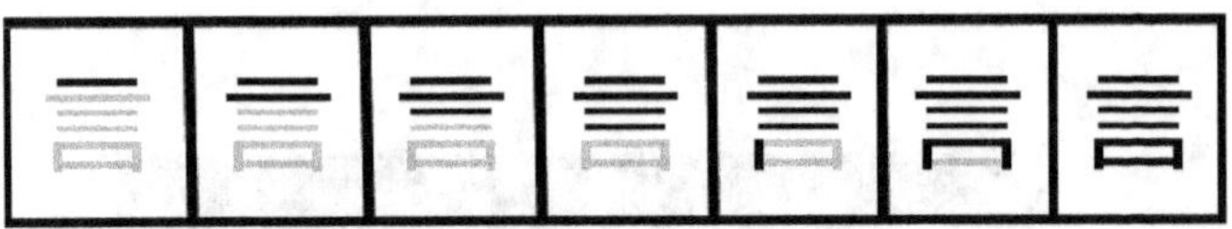

Try it:

Kun (い, こと)

言う: To say

言葉: Word, language

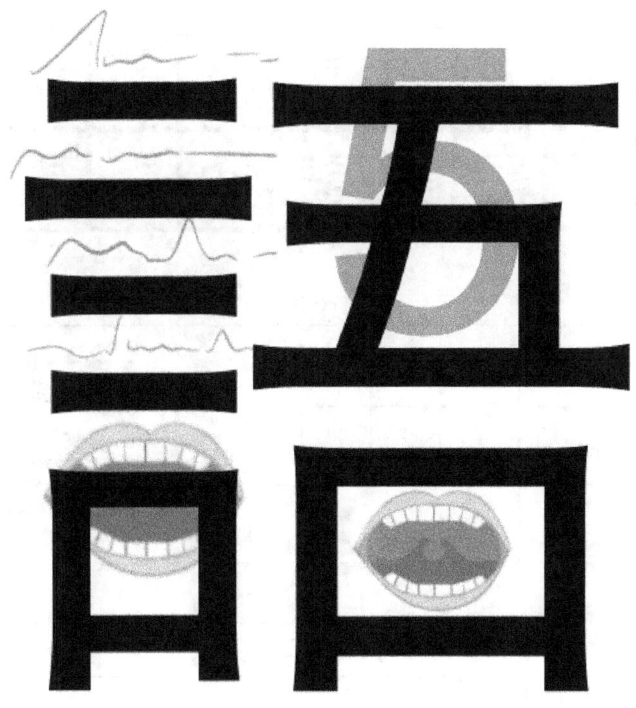

語 WORD, NARRATE

"You need more than five (五) words to narrate (語) an amazing story"

Try it:

ON (ゴ)
にほんご 日本語: Japanese language えいご 英語: English language ご 〜語: 〜language

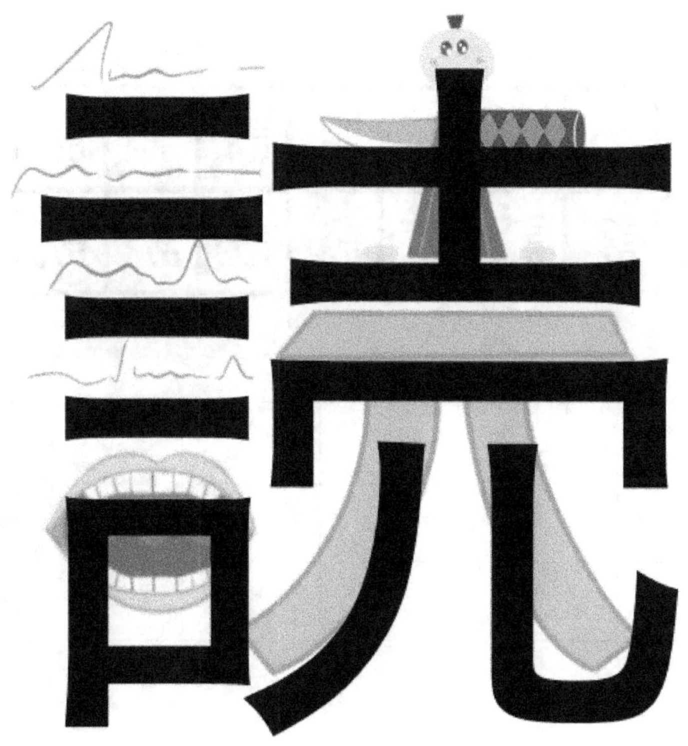

読 READ

"The samurai (士) is reading (読) the words (言) on the desk"

Try it:

Kun (よ)
よ 読む: To read

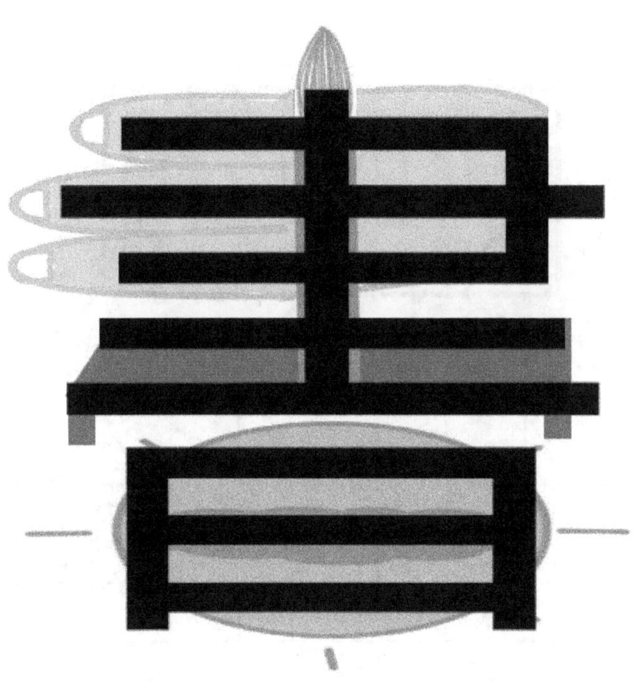

書 WRITE

"The hand holds the brush (聿) to write (書) poems about the sun (日)"

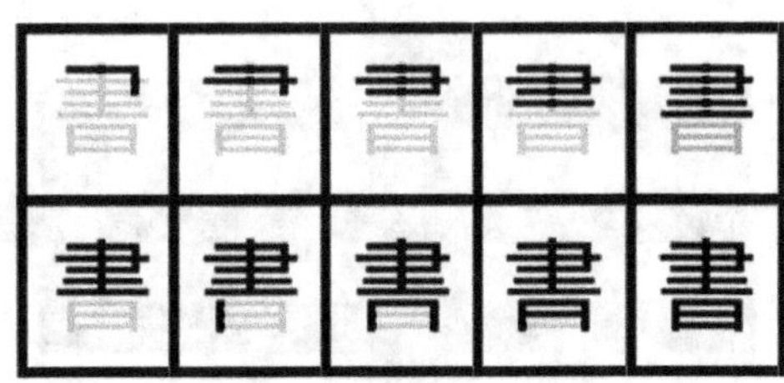

Try it:

ON (ショ)

じしょ
辞書: Dictionary

としょかん
図書館: Library

Kun (か、がき)

か
書く: To write

はがき
葉書: Postcard

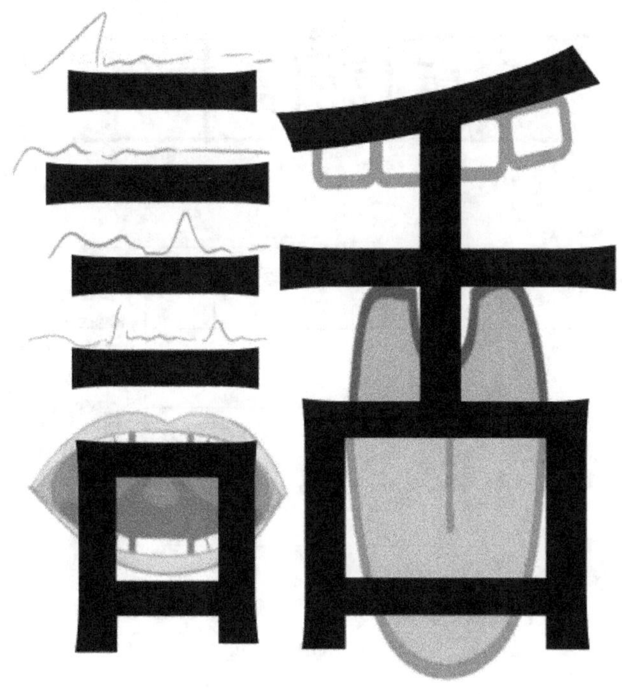

話 TALK

"The tongue (舌) is needed to talk (話)"

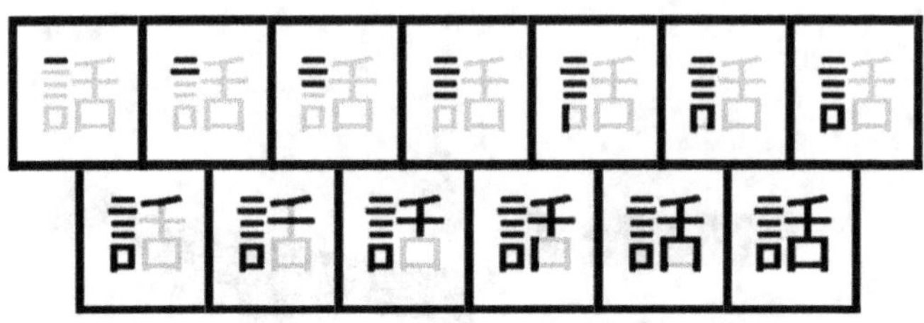

Try it:

<table>
<tr><td>ON (ワ)</td></tr>
<tr><td>でんわ
電話: Telephone</td></tr>
</table>

<table>
<tr><td>Kun (はな, はなし)</td></tr>
<tr><td>はなし
話 : Talk, story
はな
話 す: To speak</td></tr>
</table>

聞 HEAR

"The ear (耳) hears (聞) what is said between the two doors (門)"

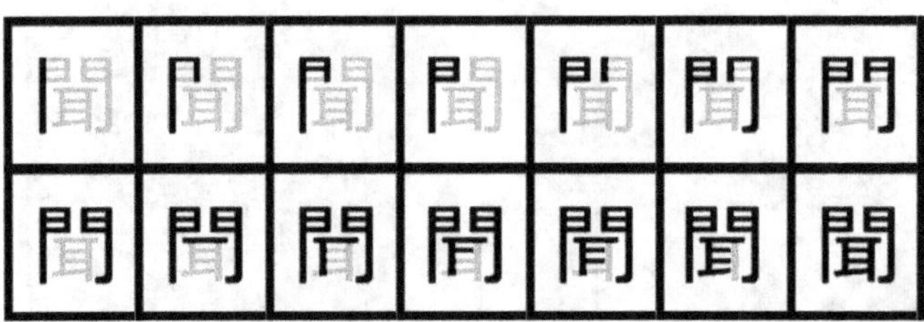

Try it:

ON (ブン)

しんぶん
新 聞 : Newspaper

Kun (き)

き
聞く : To hear, to listen to, to ask

食 EAT, FOOD

"He eats (食) delicious food under the roof"

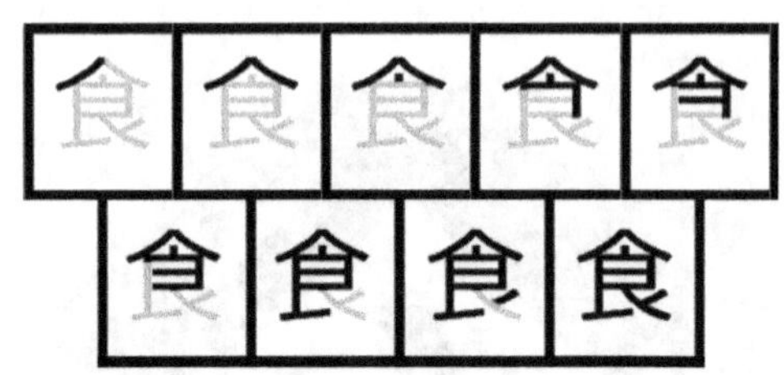

Try it:

ON (ショク)

しょくどう
食 堂 : Dining hall

Kun (たべ)

た　　もの
食べ物 : Food

た
食べる : To eat

飲 DRINK

"The thirsty man wants to drink (飲) something before eating"

Try it:

Kun (の)
の 飲む : To drink
の　　もの 飲み 物 : Beverage

立 STAND UP

"The boy stands up (立) on one leg"

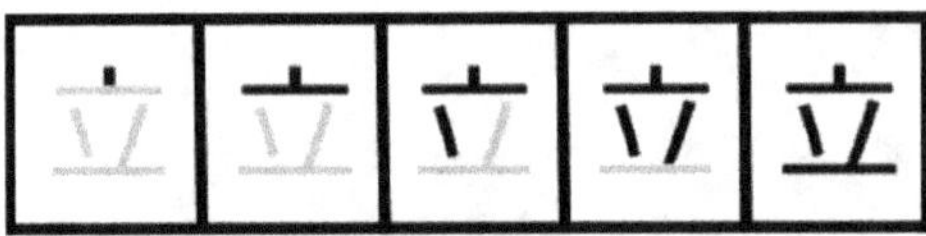

Try it:

Kun (た)
た 立つ: To stand
た 立てる: To stand (something) up

zzz…

休 REST

"The man (亻) rests (休) against the tree (木)"

休 休 休 休 休 休

Try it:

休 休

Kun (やす)

なつやす
夏 休 み: Summer holiday

やす
休 み: Rest, holiday

やす
休 む: To rest

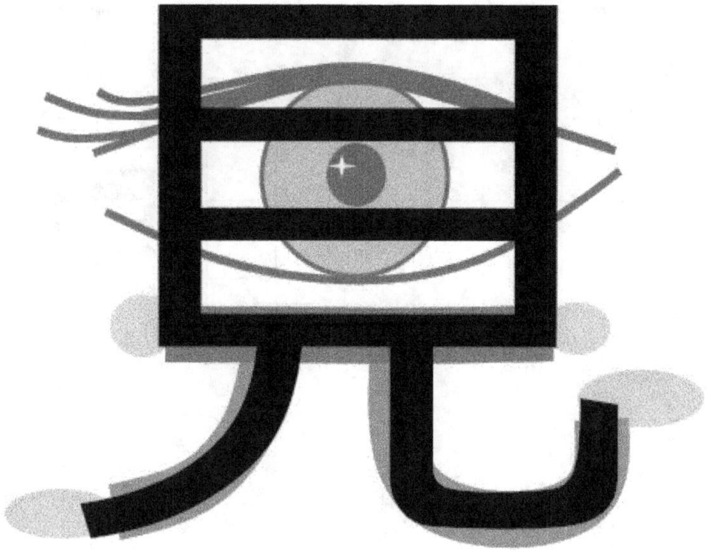

見 SEE, IDEA

"The eye (目) is ready to go (儿) and see (見) new ideas"

見 見 見 見 見 見 見

Try it:

見 見

Kun (み)
み 見る: To see, to watch
み 見せる: To show

会 MEET

"The friends meet (会) under the roof"

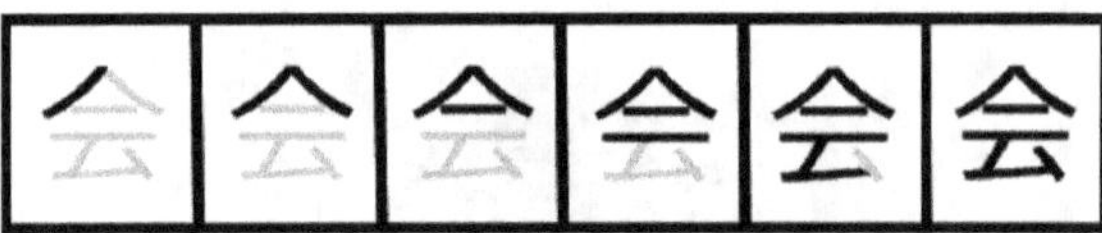

Try it:

*Note: The original kanji looked completely different and it showed the meaning of "to go on foot to meet someone"

ON (カイ)
かいしゃ 会 社 : Company

Kun (あ)
あ 会 う : To meet

学 STUDY

"When it is time to study (学), the child's (子) ideas come like fire from his head"

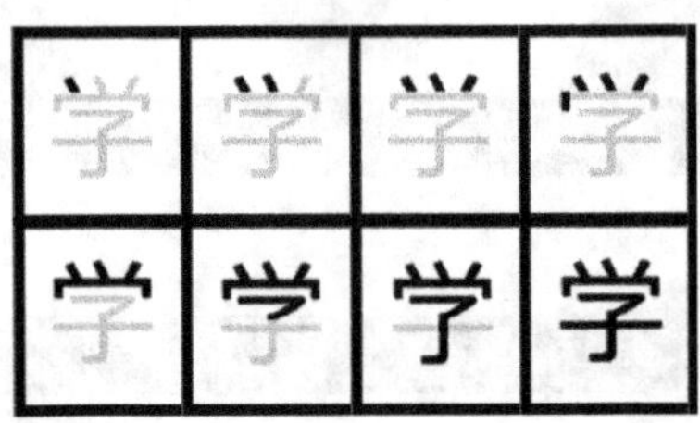

Try it:

学	学					

ON (ガク)
がくせい 学 生 : Student
がっこう 学 校 : School
だいがく 大 学 : University
りゅうがくせい 留 学 生 : Overseas student

生 LIFE, BIRTH

"The life (生) of the plant comes from the earth (土)"

Try it:

ON (セイ, ショウ)

せいと
生徒: Pupil

せんせい
先 生 : Teacher, doctor

たんじょうび
誕 生 日 : Birthday

がくせい
学 生 : Student

りゅうがくせい
留 学 生 : Overseas student

Kun (う)

う
生まれる: To be born

買 BUY

"Buying (買) a net (罒) of shells (貝) was very expensive"

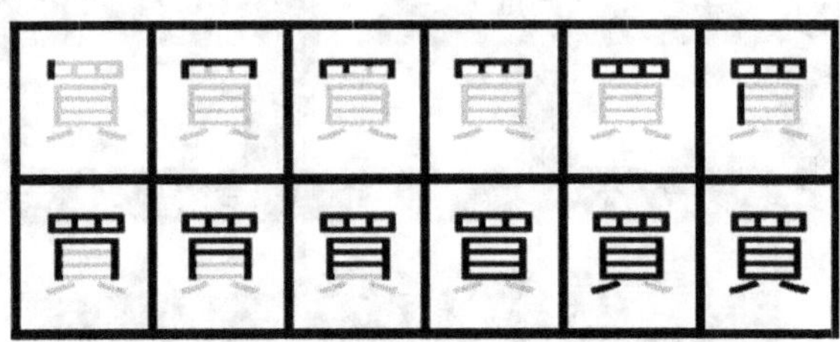

Try it:

Kun (か)
か 買う : To buy
か　　もの 買い 物 : Shopping

This book covers the 103 Kanji found in the Japanese Language Proficiency Test N5 and the main idea is to cover as much material as possible related to Kanji.
If you wish to join me in this journey of learning Japanese, check out my social media! There you can ask questions and join our conversations!

@JLPTKanjiMnemonics

Also, if you have any suggestions or improvements about my book, feel free to e-mail me at:
jlptkanjimnemonics@gmail.com

ありがとうございます！

241